LAWS THAT SHAPE OUR LIVES:
PUBLIC POLICY ESSAYS

By Matthew Howard

puma concolor aeternus press
educational series volume 4
2016

ISBN-13: 978-0692736388 (puma concolor aeternus press)
ISBN-10: 0692736387

Cover Art: *Pastel Planet #2,* © 2013 by Matthew Howard.

Chapters 3–10 previously appeared in the books *Net Neutrality for Broadband, Patents & Public Health,* and *Tobacco & Fluoride*.

Contents

Introduction

Writing about public policy presents a challenge, for the field continually changes. New laws replace old ones, court decisions overturn existing precedents, and the winds of public opinion blow first one way and then the other. So, do not consider the essays in this book as representing some permanent, unchanging state of affairs. In fact, many of the policies examined here have met with substantial resistance in legislatures and courts, both in the U.S. and abroad.

For example, the Myriad Genetics case in Chapter 7 has since been overturned by the Australian High Court on appeal from the federal court decision discussed here. This brings the Australian view of Myriad's patents more in line with the U.S. Supreme Court's. Nevertheless, you will find a comprehensive background of that case here, and a deeper understanding of its complex history.

On the other hand, Australia's policy on tobacco packaging remains intact, and as predicted here, it did "lead the pack". Similar policy has recently taken effect in the U.K. at the time of this writing, and it is meeting similar resistance from tobacco companies. Understanding the history of the Australian policy will give you a greater appreciation of how and why these packaging laws are sweeping the globe, nation by nation.

Here in the U.S., the Email Privacy Act passed unanimously in the House of Representatives is now meeting some resistance as it awaits review by the Senate Judiciary Committee. At the time of this writing, the fate of the bill remains uncertain. Both corporations and the general public have called for reforms to the laws governing how federal agencies can access customer data and business data in criminal investigations, so we can reasonably expect a change. But will this new bill be the one?

The FCC's "net neutrality" policy examined here has also met resistance, and seen some controversial application to corporate providers of broadband Internet services. While the policy does not appear to be in any immediate danger of going away, it is far from uncontested or unanimously popular.

In the same vein, few policies in the U.S. cause such emotional reactions as that of water fluoridation. Simply mentioning it tends to make people tense up and prepare to argue vehemently. I hope the fact-based research presented here will contribute to a more reasonable and level-headed discussion between both the supporters and detractors of this divisive policy.

Less divisive and perhaps more fantastic is the new realm of policy concerning exploration and mining of resources from asteroids and other celestial bodies. Many people are surprised to hear this once far-fetched topic is now a legitimate field of study for the policy analyst. The U.S. has now addressed property rights as they apply to mineral and other resources extracted from asteroids, and other countries will undoubtedly develop similar policies in the next few years.

So, while it is a challenge to write about the ever-changing realm of public policy, it is also a fascinating opportunity to take an in-depth look at the laws which affect our nation and our world. The "big picture" of the policies presented here is so big that becoming an expert on any one topic may feel impossible at first. But I hope you find these essays bring you a deeper and broader understanding of how national and international policies shape our lives, our planet, and our future.

Matthew Howard
June 2016

1

Get a Warrant:
Reforming the Electronic Communications Privacy Act in 2016

I. Introduction.

Encrypted data and user-locked devices present a challenge to federal investigators. In their attempts to access such data and devices in criminal investigations, the FBI and the Department of Justice have obtained warrants and court orders citing existing laws as giving them the authority to access the data. They have also called upon these laws to compel businesses to divulge the encryption keys which not only secure that data but the data of all the companies' customers. Recently, the FBI has even demanded Apple create new software which would unlock smart phones for them. The requests for court orders have met with mixed response from federal judges who have at times issued the orders and at times denied them. Companies have sometimes complied with these orders and other times challenged them.

The challenges include many legal and business concerns. They range from the ideas of free speech and privacy to the scope of the government's authority to coerce a business to undermine the data security at the very core of its services. These challenges are not easily dismissed, considering investigators are appealing to laws created long before the modern Internet.

For example, recent court orders involving Apple cited the All Writs Act of 1789. The FBI's attempt to use this broad law to establish authority over electronic data should come as no surprise considering the resistance Lavabit offered to the FBI's use of the Pen Register Act. That resistance resulted in contempt of court charges for Lavabit's owner and the eventual closure of the company (Silver, 2016). The Pen Register Act was created in 1986 as part of the Electronic Communications Privacy Act (ECPA), a decade before the widespread use of email and search engines. Even as amended by the Patriot Act to cover electronic and Internet communications, the ECPA suffers from applying an old way of thinking to new problems. As it currently stands, the ECPA's constitutionality is questionable for several reasons we will explore.

In April 2016, the House of Representatives took a step to correct this policy by unanimously voting in favor of H.R. 699, the Email Privacy Act. This Act would update the ECPA to require a warrant to access emails and data stored in the cloud. H.R. 699 now awaits a vote from the Senate before going to the President for enactment into law. H.R. 699 potentially solves the questions of constitutionality that arise when federal investigators access stored data without a warrant, and it also sets new boundaries about notifying customers when a service provider has been compelled to disclose the content of customers' electronic communication.

II. The ECPA: Origins and Constitutionality.

As Title III of the Electronic Communications Privacy Act of 1986 (ECPA), the Pen Register Act was passed by Congress "to provide some protection for consumers' financial records and to regulate law enforcement's use of pen registers" following the landmark privacy cases *United States v. Miller* and *Smith v. Maryland* (Lipman, 2014, p. 473). The concept of the pen register comes from the era of pre-Internet telephone communication. "A pen register records all the phone numbers dialed from a particular telephone, and a trap and trace device records all numbers that dial a specific phone number" (MacArthur, 2007, p. 448). Both of these devices are now governed by the Pen Register Act (West, p. 55).

Communication Content. But while The Pen Register Act originally applied to numbers dialed to and from a specific phone, it was amended to include modern electronic forms of communication. In 2001, the Patriot Act amended it to cover "dialing, routing, addressing, or signaling information", including "IP addresses and email addressing information" (Schwartz, 2009, p. 10). This data does not include the *content* of emails and communications, and the court's majority opinion in *Smith v. Maryland* agreed that "pen registers do not acquire the contents of communications" (Lipman, 2014, p. 475).

To access the contents of communication, rather than data about it and its users, government agencies can invoke either the Wiretap Act or Title II of the ECPA, the Stored Communications

Act. The Wiretap Act of 1968 was updated by the ECPA (U.S. DOJ, 2016). It covers communications in the process of being transmitted, such as a live phone call. But emails are transmitted quickly and are often not a live communication but an asynchronous one. For emails, transmission is "the time it takes from clicking on the 'send' command to the moment the message arrives at the server of the recipient's ISP" (Schwartz, 2009, p. 11). Therefore, statutory authority to access emails in a criminal investigation often comes from the Stored Communications Act of the ECPA. Law enforcement agencies typically seek "collection of email from ISPs [Internet Service Providers] under the Stored Communications Act," which generally has "less rigorous" requirements than the Wiretap Act (ibid). The rigorous requirement in question is a warrant.

Warrant Requirements. Accessing emails 180 days old or less requires a warrant. But under the Stored Communications Act, "opened e-mails stored for longer than 180 days can be accessed by a government official with an administrative subpoena, a grand jury subpoena, a trial subpoena, or a court order" (Lipman, 2014, p. 476). Unlike the probable cause requirement for a warrant, court orders merely require an official to show "reasonable grounds to believe that the contents... are relevant and material to an ongoing criminal investigation" (ibid).

Is the 180-day demarcation arbitrary? At least one Justice Department official believes so, having declared to the House Judiciary Committee there is "no principled basis to treat e-mail less than 180 days old differently than e-mail more than 180 days old" (Lee, 2013). Google and Yahoo agree, having stated they "require warrants for the contents of email messages or user documents stored in the cloud" regardless of the Stored Communications Act's provisions (Lipman, 2014, p. 477). Google has claimed warrantless access to communication content violates the Fourth Amendment, and "at least one Circuit Court has agreed" (ibid.) The Sixth Circuit Court, in its opinion on *United States v. Warshak*, argued that where the Stored

Communications Act allows the government warrantless access to emails, it is "unconstitutional" (6th Circuit, 2010).

The Third Party Exception. But questions about the ECPA's constitutionality go even deeper. In their attempts to access electronic communications and data about them without a warrant, federal investigators have often appealed to the "third party exception". This idea arises from the court's opinion in *Smith v. Maryland* that "individuals have no privacy interest in the information they voluntarily reveal to third parties" (Lipman, 2014, p. 475). The court's ruling has been taken to mean that by voluntarily revealing information to a service provider (the third party) to communicate, users have abandoned a reasonable expectation of privacy about the communication, and such information could therefore be obtained without a warrant.

Justice Marshall's dissenting opinion in *Smith* argued to the contrary, calling into question just how "voluntary" the reveal was to the phone company in this case. How else would a person possibly make a phone call? Marshall wrote, "It is idle to speak of 'assuming' risks in contexts where, as a practical matter, individuals have no realistic alternative" (ibid, p. 480-481). Marshall's opinion was echoed in Justice Sotomayor's concurring opinion in *United States v. Jones*, where she further argued she could not assume "all information voluntarily disclosed to some member of the public for a limited purpose is, for that reason alone, disentitled to Fourth Amendment protection" (ibid). She quoted Justice Marshall's dissent in *Smith*, where he expressed the same sentiments: "Privacy is not a discrete commodity, possessed absolutely or not at all. Those who disclose certain facts to a bank or phone company for a limited business purpose need not assume that this information will be released to other persons for other purposes."

As if to further call this third party exception into question, Congress created several laws after the *Smith v. Maryland* case, all of which contained provisions to protect privacy in some way, especially where telecommunications and banking were involved: the Right to Financial Privacy Act, the 1996 Telecommunications Act, the Pen Register Act, and the Stored Communications Act.

"Taken as a whole, these statutes enacted by Congress indicate that records released to a third-party have some constitutional privacy value." (MacArthur, 2007, p. 456-457).

Encryption and the ECPA. The scope of the ECPA was further called into question when the FBI invoked it to demand a company's SSL keys to unencrypt communications data in *United States v. Lavabit*. In the course of a criminal investigation, "the Government obtained court orders under both the Pen/Trap Statute... and the Stored Communications Act" (4th Circuit, 2014, p. 4). "Lavabit employed two stages of encryption for its paid subscribers: storage encryption and transport encryption" (ibid, p. 5-6). In other words, Lavabit's service encrypted both stored emails and emails in the process of transmission, and the encryption covered not just the contents but non-content data about the emails.

When Lavabit contested the original orders, more court orders were issued until the FBI was first demanding they receive unencrypted data and eventually demanding the SSL (Secure Socket Layers) keys (ibid, p. 9-12). Lavabit used five key-pairs, one for each email protocol it supported, and the Court of Appeals' decision admits that if even one private key-pair became "anything less than private" it could "affect all of Lavabit's estimated 400,000-plus email users" (ibid p. 7-8). The district court was well aware that the keys would "practically enable the Government" to "collect all users' data" (ibid, p. 17). Lavabit attempted to negotiate these orders with proposals that included limiting the duration of the register's installation, requesting payments for the unencryption services, and offering to unencrypt certain metadata relevant to the investigation before giving it to the FBI.

But, having had enough of Lavabit's delays, "the Government obtained a seizure warrant from the District Court under the Stored Communications Act" which demanded all "information necessary to decrypt communications sent to or from (the target's) Lavabit email account... including encryption and SSL keys" (ibid, p. 13). The warrant is important because it sought to clarify something about the court orders which remained in question; namely, did the Pen/Trap Order provide sufficient authority to compel Lavabit to hand over its encryption keys? "The district court observed that the Pen/Trap Order's 'technical assistance' provision may or may not encompass the keys, but it declined to reach the issue during the show cause hearing" because the search warrant had been issued (ibid, p. 14). "The government agreed that it had sought the seizure warrant to 'avoid litigating [the] issue' of whether the Pen/Trap Order reached the encryption keys" despite having contended that it did (ibid p.14-15).

Lavabit did eventually hand over the keys, first in the form of an "11-page printout containing largely illegible characters in 4-point type" and then, at the investigators' insistence, in an "industry-standard electronic format" (ibid, p. 17-18). But the process raises the question of whether or not the Pen Register Act's provision mandating the company provide technical assistance during the register's court-ordered installation could be broadly expanded to include handing over encryption keys which could render vulnerable the data for all users of the service. The Court of Appeals declined to reach a clear verdict on this question, finding it immaterial to the question of whether or not Lavabit was in contempt, and further finding that Lavabit had not sufficiently raised this question prior to the appeal.

We are left with a judicially unresolved question about the scope of court orders under the ECPA. Do they contain sufficient authority to do more than simply monitor or access data? Do they also contain authority to compel companies to hand over the encryption keys which are at the very heart of the secure communications service they provide to all their users? The FBI's obtaining a warrant to get the keys suggests the court orders do *not* have such authority, and the FBI's reticence to litigate this point suggests they know this. The case further suggests that a seizure warrant does have this authority. This point will become relevant when we examine the new provisions of H.R. 699 which require warrants.

III. The All Writs Act and Apple.

Encrypted data is not the only security measuring frustrating federal law enforcement agencies. Devices locked with user-created passwords or codes also prevent access to the data they hold. Recently, the FBI has attempted to use the All Writs Act of 1789 to force Apple to help them unlock iPhones. Though not a part of the ECPA, the All Writs Act is worth examining briefly, for the public debate over the Apple incidents contributed to the privacy and due process concerns which spurred congressional reformation of the ECPA. It also highlights the tension over accessing data without a warrant, for the "writs" in question are court orders.

The All Writs Act, predating the invention of the phonograph by nearly 100 years, is perhaps an unusual law to invoke in matters of electronic communication. It simply states, "The Supreme Court and all courts established by Act of Congress may issue all writs necessary or appropriate in aid of their respective jurisdictions and agreeable to the usages and principles of law" (28 U.S. Code § 1651-Writs). This broad and somewhat vague language allows federal investigators to invoke the Act, but that same language calls its constitutionality and applicability into question.

Demanding New Software. Pursuant to the FBI's request in the course of a criminal investigation, Sheri Pym, a United States Magistrate Judge for the Central District of California, ordered Apple to create "a new software bundle" to load onto the suspect's iPhone (Davidson, 2016). The FBI sought this court order to give it access to a phone "locked by a user-determined, numeric passcode" (U.S. District Court, 2016). Apple has complied with past court orders to help extract information from iPhones; however, the operating system (iOS9) on this phone was created with no "back door" for bypassing the security measure (Davidson, 2016).

The software ordered would need to be digitally signed by Apple so the phone would recognize it as legitimate software (Yadron, 2016). Articles in the press voiced a fear that if the FBI had software signed by Apple, it could potentially send out software updates to any iPhone on the planet. "For instance, if the FBI were able to intercept the net connection of a target (known as a 'man in the middle' attack), with Apple's private key it could plausibly push an update that looked like a real software release from the company" (Hern, 2016). The FBI demanded that Apple create new software the FBI could load on the phone to gain access and enter passcodes electronically instead of using the touch screen, with a request that it only work on that phone rather than all iPhones (Davidson, 2016). Whether or not this exclusivity was technologically feasible was a matter of debate.

Apple had already provided assistance to the FBI in this case. Apple accessed the phone's backup in iCloud and provided all its data on the user to the FBI; however, the backups ended six weeks before the crime under investigation took place (Yadron, 2016). Apple's voluntary assistance ended when the FBI asked for the new software. Apple objected to creating a new means of bypassing its own security protocols for its product. Such a move would undermine the company's products and services, and this is no small objection. Apple's business faced a threat much like the one which ultimately destroyed Lavabit and also damaged a Lavabit rival (Hushmail) when it complied with a similar FBI request in 2007 (Rushe, 2014). Court orders which threaten to destroy a business might be defended against as "unreasonable" (ibid).

Questions of Authority. Does the All Writs Act give courts authority to compel businesses to create such software? If it does, then Apple had a legal obligation to comply, or at least attempt to. But the language of the All Writs Act is vague and open to interpretation. Was the new software "necessary", "appropriate", and "agreeable to the usage and principles of law"?

The FBI's request certainly *appeared* necessary to the District Court Magistrate, who was convinced by the FBI's claim that "Apple has the exclusive technical means which would assist the government" (U.S. District Court, 2016). But it turns out to have not been necessary at all. The FBI got what they wanted via an undisclosed third party using an undisclosed method (Selyukh,

2016). Contrary to the FBI's assertion, Apple clearly held no "exclusive means" to get the data. In fact, the FBI had the technological means to try every possible four-digit code, but it would have taken a long time—possibly thousands of hours (Davidson, 2016). Therefore, the FBI sought something that was not *necessary*, but merely *expedient*.

The appropriateness of the FBI's request remains disputed. In a similar investigation in February 2016, James Orenstein, a United States Magistrate Judge for the Eastern District of New York, rejected a similar Department of Justice request made under the All Writs Act. When the FBI wanted to order Apple to unlock an accused drug dealer's phone, Judge Orenstein argued that "the All Writs Act (AWA) can't be used to order a technology company to manipulate its products," and that the implications of applying the Act in this way would "produce impermissibly absurd results" (Ackerman, February 2016). He argued that issuing the order would be "in such tension of the doctrine of separation of powers" that it would "cast doubt on the AWA's constitutionality" (ibid). Unconstitutional and absurd do not sound appropriate.

What about agreeableness to usage and principles of law? Frankly, no one knows. The All Writs Act was last used 1977 to compel a telecommunications company to allow the FBI to install two phone lines to surveil other specific phone lines under investigation (Shahani, 2016). In this action, the telco was not tasked with creating any new hardware or software, so it does not establish a clear principle of law relevant to the Apple order. Instead, executive agencies are asking federal judges to base court orders on a vague statute that establishes no clear limits on the government's authority to compel action in its investigations.

Taken altogether, these questions cast doubt on the All Writs Act as a source of legal authority in these matters. But for the sake of argument, let us accept the position that companies *should* be compelled to create new software to circumvent their own security and encryption protocols, and to give that software to federal investigators. Then, we either need to base a request for a court order on some other statute, or we need Congress to create a new statue.

Members of Congress from both parties expressed this viewpoint when the House Judiciary Committee reviewed the Apple order and heard testimonies from both sides (Ackerman, March 2016). The solution is *not* asking the judiciary to establish legal precedent in the absence of detailed legislation. The solution is asking Congress to define the reasonable limits of personal security and national security at stake. Congress holds the responsibility of establishing a clear legal authority, and the All Writs Act is not it.

IV. H.R. 699 and Reforming the ECPA.

Given the public uproar, corporate resistance, and mixed judicial response in the cases thus far discussed, it makes sense for Congress to establish clearer legislative guidelines. Both the legislature and the general public appear to agree with the American Civil Liberties Union which said, "Online privacy law shouldn't be older than the Web, and Americans shouldn't have to choose between technology and privacy" (ACLU, 2016). Or, as Google declares in their Transparency Report, the ECPA "was passed in 1986, before the web as we know it even existed. It has failed to keep pace with how people use the Internet today" (Google, 2016).

Now, Congress has taken action. On April 27, the House of Representatives unanimously voted in favor of H.R. 699, the Email Privacy Act (Skley, 2016). This follows a unanimous agreement by the House Judiciary Committee to advance the bill for a vote (Center, 2016). Enjoying bipartisan support, the bill now moves to the Senate.

Notifying Investigated Parties. A suit recently filed by Microsoft challenges the existing ECPA in another way that is relevant to this new legislation. *Microsoft Corp v. United States Department of Justice*, filed in the U.S. District Court, Western District of Washington, made headlines only two weeks before the House voted on H.R. 699. Microsoft seeks the right to notify its customers when federal agencies request access to customer emails and data (McBride, 2016). Microsoft argues, "People do not give up their rights when they move their private information from physical storage to the cloud" (ibid). This argument echoes the increasing public concern about federal agencies' accessing electronic communications data without the knowledge of the parties under investigation, a practice which arguably contravenes Fourth Amendment rights.

H.R. 699 includes a provision specifically addressing Microsoft's concern by allowing companies to notify their subscribers "of a receipt of warrant, court order, subpoena", or other types of requests specified in the bill. It does, however, create an exception in section 2705, the delayed notice provision. The bill permits delaying notification of up to 180 days if it may be "reasonably believed" to potentially result in five conditions: flight from prosecution, witness intimidation, jeopardizing the investigation, destroying or tampering with the device, and threats to a person's physical safety. This is a significant change for the ECPA, which has allowed not only a ninety-day delay in notification, but "indefinite ninety-day extensions available by court order, as long as notification would seriously jeopardize an investigation or unduly delay a trial" (Lipman, 2014, p. 476).

Stricter Warrant Requirements. But H.R. 699 goes even further, addressing the concerns raised when agencies use the third party exception to access data without a warrant. H.R. 699 "would require a warrant to obtain the content of emails, online documents, and other private electronic communications," and "creates no special carve-outs for federal civil agencies" (Center, 2016). This is an important change, because the threshold for granting a warrant under the ECPA is higher than that for a court order, which is in turn higher than a subpoena. Warrants under the ECPA are currently only available for criminal investigations.

This new requirement for a warrant appears in Section 3, "Amendments to Required Disclosure". With a few exceptions, this section requires governmental agencies to obtain a warrant from a federal or state court before requesting the "contents of wire or electronic communications in electronic storage with or otherwise stored, held, or maintained by" a service provider. H.R. 699 then extends this same requirement where "remote computing services" are concerned.

However, these mandates for a warrant only apply to the *contents* of the communication. "Subscriber or customer information" may be disclosed by non-warrant means such as "an administrative subpoena authorized by federal or state statute, a grand jury, trial, or civil discovery subpoena". In these instances where subscriber data is disclosed without disclosing the contents of the communications, H.R. 699 does not require notifying the customer. This subscriber information includes name, address, local and long distance telephone connection records, records of session times and durations, length of service (including start date), types of service used, telephone or instrument number, any temporarily assigned network address, and the means and source of payment for services (including credit card or bank account number).

H.R. 699 also clarifies, in the section "Rule of Construction of Legal Process", that the government can use any of the non-warrant methods to require the "originator, addressee, or intended recipient" to disclose the contents of a communication. In other words, people sending and receiving the communication can be compelled to disclose the contents, though the service provider cannot (without a warrant, at least). The same applies to persons or entities who provide communications *and* who own the communications system itself. This seems to admit that if a communicator owns the communication system, that system is not a third party and may be considered differently by investigators. The non-warrant methods also apply to persons or entities when the communication "promotes a product or service" and has "been made readily accessible to the general public". In other words, advertisements.

Another notable exception involves Congress itself. Congress enjoys the power to compel disclosures in its investigations (the power of inquiry, per Article I of the Constitution). This bill will not restrict that power. Congress, though not law enforcement or other governmental agencies, can still compel the disclosure of the contents of stored communications from persons or entities under investigation *by Congress.*

And finally, H. R. 699 explicitly states that nothing about this bill limits the provisions of the Wiretap Act and the Foreign Intelligence Surveillance Act of 1978. This potentially leaves a wide-open door for the kinds of secret surveillance activities which have made headlines the past few years, particularly by the National Security Agency (NSA). It was, after all, the Foreign Intelligence Surveillance Court that granted the court order allowing the NSA to obtain Verizon's call data (Greenwald, 2013).

V. Conclusion.

Overall, the pending Email Privacy Act appears to be an improvement for all parties involved. It clarifies the procedure for the executive branch by drawing a distinct boundary about what can be obtained by court order versus a warrant. This provides a stronger and clearer rule for the judiciary who must both issue the warrants and decide cases where the scope and authority of court orders come into question. And it is a winning move for the legislature which has proven responsive to the pressure from the general public, the corporate sector, and the other branches to craft more clearly defined and technologically relevant legislation on matters of electronic communication. The ECPA has become increasingly outdated as technology advances, and this update is well overdue.

On the other hand, the Email Privacy Act still allows for a great measure of secrecy in its delayed notification provisions and its unwillingness to address matters that fall under the Foreign Intelligence Surveillance Act. It may also receive criticism for continuing to allow access to metadata merely by court order and not by warrant. It does, however, take a major step in clearing up questions over the legality and constitutionality of accessing metadata versus content.

At the very least, the public will have a firm legal basis for expecting privacy regarding the content of electronic communications and the content of documents stored in the cloud. And, both citizens and their corporate service providers will have a clear expectation about when customers will or will not be notified when agencies request access to their data. While it may not be hailed as a perfect solution by all parties, it achieves its stated goal of improving privacy protections, and it will clear up legal questions which have plagued the judiciary and the executive since the dawn of the Internet.

References

Ackerman, Spencer, et. al. (29 February, 2016). "Apple Case: Judge Rejects FBI Request for Access to Drug Dealer's iPhone." *The Guardian*. https://www.theguardian.com/technology/2016/feb/29/apple-fbi-case-drug-dealer-iphone-jun-feng-san-bernardino

Ackerman, Spencer, et. al. (1 March, 2016). "Congress Tells FBI that Forcing Apple to Unlock iPhones is 'a Fool's Errand'." *The Guardian*. https://www.theguardian.com/technology/2016/mar/01/apple-fbi-congress-hearing-iphone-encryption-san-bernardino

American Civil Liberties Union (ACLU). (2016). "It's Time for a Privacy Update." https://www.aclu.org/infographic/its-time-privacy-update?redirect=technology-and-liberty/its-time-privacy-update

Center for Democracy & Technology. (2016, April 13). "ECPA Reform Takes a Leap Forward: Email Privacy Act to Receive a Vote." https://cdt.org/press/ecpa-reform-takes-a-leap-forward-email-privacy-act-to-receive-a-vote/

Davidson, Amy. (19 February, 2016). "The Dangerous All Writs Act Precedent in the Apple Encryption Case." *The New Yorker*. http://www.newyorker.com/news/amy-davidson/a-dangerous-all-writ-precedent-in-the-apple-case

Google. (2016). "Google Transparency Report: User Data Requests." https://www.google.com/transparencyreport/userdatarequests/legalprocess/#whats_the_difference

Greenwald, Glenn. (2013, June 6). "NSA Collecting Phone Records of Millions of Verizon Customers Daily." *The Guardian*.

http://www.theguardian.com/world/2013/jun/06/nsa-phone-records-verizon-court-order

Hern, Alex. (2016, March 11). "FBI 'Could Force Apple to Hand over Private Key'." *The Guardian*. https://www.theguardian.com/technology/2016/mar/11/fbi-could-force-apple-to-hand-over-private-key

H.R. 699. *The Email Privacy Act*. https://www.congress.gov/bill/114th-congress/house-bill/699/text

Lee, Timothy B. (16 May, 2013). "Eric Holder Endorses Warrants for E-mail. It's About Time." *Washington Post*. http://www.washingtonpost.com/blogs/wonkblog/wp/2013/05/16/eric-holder-endorses-warrants-for-e-mail-its-about-time/

Lipman, Rebecca. (2014). "The Third Party Exception: Reshaping an Imperfect Doctrine for the Digital Age." *Harvard Law & Policy Review, 8*(2): 471-490.

MacArthur, Andrew P. (2007, Spring). "The NSA Phone Call Database: The Problematic Acquisition and Mining of Call Records in the United States, Canada, the United Kingdom, and Australia." *Duke Journal of Comparative & International Law, 17*(2): 441-481. http://scholarship.law.duke.edu/cgi/viewcontent.cgi?article=1086&context=djcil

McBride, Sarah. (2016, April 15). "Microsoft Sues U.S. Government over Data Requests." *Reuters*. http://www.reuters.com/article/us-microsoft-privacy-idUSKCN0XB22U

Rushe, Dominic. (2014, February 1). "Lawyers for Lavabit Founder: Judges May Dismiss Civil Liberties Concerns." *The Guardian*.

https://www.theguardian.com/technology/2014/feb/01/lavabit
-ladar-levison-snowden-contempt-court

Schwartz, Paul M. (2009, Sep.). "Keeping Track of
Telecommunications Surveillance." *Communications of the
ACM, 52*(9): 24-26.

Selyukh, Alina. (29 March, 2016). "Apple Vs. the FBI: The
Unanswered Questions and Unsettled Issues." *National Public
Radio (NPR).*
http://www.npr.org/sections/alltechconsidered/2016/03/29/4
72141323/apple-vs-the-fbi-the-unanswered-questions-and-
unsettled-issues

Shahani, Aarti. (21 March, 2016). "How a Gambling Case Does,
and Doesn't, Apply to the iPhone Debate." *National Public
Radio (NPR).*
http://www.npr.org/sections/alltechconsidered/2016/03/21/47
1312150/how-a-gambling-case-does-and-doesnt-apply-to-the-
iphone-debate

Silver, Joe. (2106, April 14). "Lavabit Held in Contempt of Court
for Printing Crypto Key in Tiny Font [Updated]." *ArsTechnica.*
http://arstechnica.com/tech-policy/2014/04/lavabit-held-in-
contempt-of-court-for-printing-crypto-key-in-tiny-font/

Skley, Dennis. (2016, April 27). "U.S. House Unanimously Passed
Bill Requiring Warrants for E-mail." *ArsTechnica.*
http://arstechnica.com/tech-policy/2016/04/us-house-
unanimously-passed-bill-requiring-warrants-for-e-mail/

United States Code. 18 U.S. Code § 206. *Pen Registers and Trap
and Trace Devices.*
https://www.law.cornell.edu/uscode/text/18/part-II/chapter-
206

United States Code. 28 U.S.C. § 1651. *The All Writs Act.*
https://www.law.cornell.edu/uscode/text/28/1651#a

United States Department of Justice. *Electronic Communications Privacy Act of 1986 (ECPA), 18 USC 2510-22.* (Informational summary of the ECPA.)
https://it.ojp.gov/PrivacyLiberty/authorities/statutes/1285

United States District Court for the Central District of California. (16 February, 2016). ED No. 15-0451M, *Government's Ex Parte Application for Order Compelling Apple Inc. to Assist Agents in Search; Memorandum of Points and Authorities; Declaration of Christopher Pluhar; Exhibit.* (The original request for the order in question.)
https://www.washingtonpost.com/news/volokh-conspiracy/wp-content/uploads/sites/14/2016/02/AWAApplication.pdf

United States Court of Appeals for the Fourth Circuit. (2014). Appeal 13-4625 in *United States v. Lavabit.* Judge G. Steven Agee joined by Judge Paul Niemeyer and Judge Roger Gregory. http://pdfserver.amlaw.com/nlj/lavabit-usca4-op.pdf

United States Court of Appeals for the Sixth Circuit. (2010). *United States v. Warshak,* 631 F.3d 266, 286 (Qtd in Lipman, 2014, p. 477).

West Legal Studies in Business, a Division of Thomson Learning. "Pen Register Act." *Privacy, Slide 55.* INT 658 Law of Cyberspace, Course Materials.

Yadron, Danny, et. al. (21 February, 2016). "FBI Told San Bernardino County Staff to Tamper with Gunman's Apple Account." *The Guardian.*
https://www.theguardian.com/technology/2016/feb/20/san-bernadino-county-fbi-gunman-apple-account

2

Beyond This Horizon:
Understanding the Political and Economic Context of the U.S. Commercial Space Launch Competitiveness Act

Abstract

The U.S. Commercial Space Launch Competitiveness Act, signed into law in November 2015, brought the world the first national policy to grant citizens and companies property rights to resources they can extract from asteroids and other objects in space. The Act takes care to remain consistent with existing international treaties, aligning with the Outer Space Treaty and contrasting with the more cooperative but failed Moon Treaty. The Act further mandates the development of national policies to address safety, launch coordination, and commercial partnerships. It requires a number of reports and assessments due in 2016 from various agencies, especially the Secretary of Transportation. The National Oceanic and Atmospheric Administration issued new policy in early 2016 to address partnering with the commercial sector on space missions, and the nation of Luxembourg has begun developing its own national policy on these matters of property rights and commercial partnerships. An economically viable asteroid mining industry will depend on the development not only of new technologies, but on the creation of a space-based economy using the extracted resources for propellants and construction in space. Collaborative partnerships between the governmental, commercial, and academic sectors will be a driving force in making this economy possible.

Keywords: Academic Sector, Asteroid Exploration, Asteroid Mining, Commercial Space Exploration, Extracted Resources, H.R. 2262, NASA, Outer Space Treaty, Property Rights, Public Policy, Private Sector, Space-Based Resources, Space-Based Economy, U.S. Commercial Space Launch Competitiveness Act

I. Introduction.

In November 2015, President Obama signed into law H.R. 2262, The U.S. Commercial Space Launch Competitiveness Act. This Act provides new clarity about private U.S. citizens' property rights concerning resources extracted from asteroids and other objects in space. Multiple private companies are planning their own commercial space travel, exploration, and extraterrestrial mining operations in the next few years, giving birth to an industry unlike anything in history. With a new industry come new opportunities for policy makers to address the legal, political, and economic concerns uniquely raised by the industry, as well as opportunities to encourage the technological developments required to make that industry grow. H.R. 2262 positions the USA as a policy leader in defining rights to space-based resources to stimulate commercial involvement in the embryonic industry of asteroid mining, and sets the stage for a global movement towards making this industry a significant economic force by fostering collaboration between the governmental, commercial, and academic sectors.

Part One: Politics and Property Rights in the Context of International Law.

II. H.R. 2262 Title IV—Space Resource Exploration and Utilization Act of 2015.

H.R. 2262 addresses many space-related concerns in its brief nineteen pages. We first consider its Title IV which has given private industry the greatest cause for celebration. In a globally unprecedented move, the U.S. has addressed the concept of property rights as they apply to resources extracted from objects in space. The scope and meaning of Title IV requires an understanding of the international treaty environment which carries obligations for the U.S.

The Corporation as Citizen. One thing must be made clear from the beginning. Title IV uses the term "United States citizen". To avoid confusion over whether or not this language applies to private companies and corporations, H.R. 2262 defines "United States Citizen" per the United States Code, Title 51, Section 50902. That document defines a "citizen of the United States" as one of three things: "an **individual** who is a citizen of the United States"; "an **entity** organized or existing under the laws of the United States or a State"; "or an entity organized or existing under the laws of a foreign country if the controlling interest (as defined by the Secretary of Transportation) is held by" one of the two previously named types of citizens. For the purposes of H.R. 2262, corporations are included in statements about citizens.

Private Property Rights. After a brief Section 51301 which provides definitions, Section 51302 authorizes the President to encourage "commercial exploration" and "commercial recovery of space resources by United States citizens". It authorizes the President to "discourage government barriers" to developing economically viable industries for these purposes. This section requires the President to "submit to Congress a report" recommending how responsibilities on this matter will be allocated to federal agencies. This report is due within 180 days of the bill's enactment, placing its deadline in May 2016.

Next, Section 51303 "Asteroid resource and space resource rights" gets to the heart of the matter. In its entirety, it reads:

"A United States citizen engaged in commercial recovery of an asteroid resource or a space resource under this chapter shall be entitled to any asteroid resource or space resource obtained, including to possess, own, transport, use, and sell the asteroid resource or space resource obtained in accordance with applicable law, including the international obligations of the United States."

Representative Brian Babin (R-TX), Chairman of the Space subcommittee of the House Committee on Science, addressed concerns over these international obligations in a speech to the

10th Eilene Galloway Symposium on Critical Issues in Space Law in December, 2015 (Planetary Resources, 2015). According to Babin, Title IV is:

"...consistent with U.S. international obligations. Article VI of the Outer Space Treaty explicitly recognizes that non-governmental entities, such as private corporations, may explore and use outer space, including the right to remove, take possession, and use in-situ natural resources from celestial bodies" (Babin, 2015).

It is also "consistent with United States obligations under Article II of the Outer Space Treaty and is not an assertion of sovereignty or jurisdiction over any celestial body" (ibid). Representative Babin clarifies here the intention of the final paragraph of Title IV, which states the U.S. "does not assert sovereignty or sovereign or exclusive rights or jurisdiction over, or the ownership of, any celestial body." Examining these treaties further illuminates the new law.

III. Treaties and International Law.

The Outer Space Treaty: Existing Treaty Obligations. The Outer Space Treaty, first created in 1967, is formally called the *Treaty on Principles Governing the Activities of States in the Exploration and Use of Outer Space, including the Moon and Other Celestial Bodies.* Some language in the treaty suggests a cooperative approach to space-based resources, that they should be used for the benefit of everyone on Earth. For example, Article I states,

"The exploration and use of outer space, including the moon and other celestial bodies, shall be carried out for the benefit and in the interests of all countries, irrespective of their degree of economic or scientific development, and shall be the province of all mankind" (Treaty, 1967).

Article IX of the Outer Space Treaty includes language about the well-being of other nations, such as:

"States Parties to the Treaty shall pursue studies of outer space, including the moon and other celestial bodies, and conduct exploration of them so as to avoid their harmful contamination and also adverse changes in the environment of the earth resulting from the introduction of extraterrestrial matter".

However, the Outer Space Treaty does not address ownership of extracted resources, or any obligation to share them with other nations. Article IV only says "that non-governmental organisations have to be supervised by their nation states", a clause which creates a "compromise" giving "private companies a chance to exploit the new frontier" of space-based resources (Brooks, 2014, p. 26). H.R. 2262 builds on this idea that claiming ownership of areas, such as a parcel of land on the Moon, is not allowed, but ownership may attach to the extracted resources, even by commercial companies. H.R. 2262 aims to stimulate a competitive environment where private enterprise stands to gain a financial stake in extracting resources from space. To those who would argue for the ideals embodied in a more cooperative environment of sharing those resources with all nations, it is worth examining the failure of another treaty which sought exactly that: the Moon Treaty.

The Moon Treaty versus Profit Motives. The Moon Treaty, formally titled *The Agreement Governing the Activities of States on the Moon and Other Celestial Bodies,* has gathered only seven signatory nations since its creation in 1979 (Agreement, 1979). Put simply, "The seven nations which have ratified the Moon Agreement have no investment in it—they are not space-faring" (Brooks, 2014, p. 26). Within its twenty-one articles, the treaty includes such noble language as "the moon and its natural resources are the common heritage of mankind" and requires that "all space vehicles, equipment, facilities, stations and installations on the moon shall be open to other States Parties." It also advocates sharing of extracted resources between nations:

"An equitable sharing by all States Parties in the benefits derived from those resources, whereby the interests and needs of the developing countries, as well as the efforts of those countries which have contributed either directly or indirectly to the exploration of the moon, shall be given special consideration" (Agreement, 1979).

The authors of *Space Mineral Resources* agree the Outer Space Treaty, being the most widely ratified, is the dominant space treaty, and the Moon Treaty was a "failure" because it sought to "systematically prohibit the profit motive that so many societies see as their life's blood" (Dula, 2015). The lack of signatory nations suggests the Treaty's focus on cooperation, equitable sharing, and global consideration of developing nations does not appear attractive to the more developed space-faring nations. It stands in stark contrast to the private-ownership provisions of H.R. 2262. *Space Mineral Resources* argues that the "common heritage of mankind" concept—that the use and benefits of space-based resources belong to all humans equally and should be shared—is unlikely to become an enforceable policy given the failure of the Moon Treaty (ibid). Whether or not one believes that believes space-based resources *should* be shared by all humanity, such an international agreement about property rights in space stands very little chance of being ratified.

H.R. 2622 evidences a belief that competition between private citizens will create the economic incentive necessary to encourage asteroid mining. When speaking of lunar exploration and usage, Bigelow Aerospace attorney Mike Gold told *Dissent* magazine, "Property rights are key to gaining the investment necessary to move forward" (Riederer, 2014, p. 8). Title IV of H.R. 2262 embodies this thinking, assigning property rights to private citizens for their extracted resources, while simultaneously denying any ownership or sovereign claims to celestial bodies themselves.

Sovereignty, Jurisdiction, and Customary International Law. If that sounds potentially complicated, Michael Simpson, executive director of the Secure World Foundation, an "organization dedicated to the sustainable use of space resources", agrees: "In recorded history, we have never dealt with a system of governance, whether formal or informal, in the absence of sovereignty" (Riederer, 2014, p. 10). What exactly is meant by "sovereignty"?

The Encyclopædia Britannica defines sovereignty as "the ultimate... authority in the decision-making process of the state", noting the modern meaning of "absolute authority to declare the law" stems from the works of philosopher Thomas Hobbes (Encyclopædia, 2014). Therefore, an absence of sovereignty in space means no single nation may be the ultimate source of laws or authority in space or on celestial bodies. However, this concept does not relegate human activity in space to an environment of lawless anarchy, for nations do have jurisdiction over their citizens in space, as well as having guiding principles of international law to consider.

The Outer Space Treaty addresses jurisdiction using a rationale similar to the United Nations Convention on Law of the Sea (Dula, 2015). While a nation cannot lay claim to a celestial body as its territory, the nation's laws govern its citizens upon it. This concept is called quasi-territorial jurisdiction. It is the same concept that binds a nation's citizens to that nation's laws when they are at sea, outside the recognized geographic borders of the nation.

The authors of *Space Mineral Resources* also explore the concept of Customary International Law (CIL), which is the area where norms become binding to some degree, whether through general established practice or general legal opinions. The authors predict a relatively new development in CIL, where commercial, non-governmental companies play a major role in establishing those norms and general practices, simply by virtue of the major role they will play in this new frontier (Dula, 2015). This could be a cautionary note to policy makers, lest the absence of a strong legal framework allows commercial enterprise to define public law.

IV. The Future of Public Policy on Asteroid Mining.

H.R. 2262 and Public Safety. Safety remains an important public policy matter where private space launches and exploration are concerned. The Outer Space Treaty comes from the days when the U.S. and U.S.S.R. were the dominant players, and the Moon was the main target. Now, policy makers face a potentially complex and unsafe environment, a multitude of individual commercial missions with their own agendas and timetables. The authors of *Space Mineral Resources* proposed creating a "Space Traffic Control Center" to coordinate traffic, time launches, and reduce the possibility of collisions and disasters (Dula, 2015).

H.R. 2262 does not offer definitive safety guidelines, but it sets the wheels in motion to establish them. Title I addresses the need for safety in Sections 108-111, requiring reports from the Secretary of Transportation in consultation with NASA, the FCC, the Secretary of State, the Secretary of Commerce, the Secretary of Defense, the Commercial Space Transportation Advisory Committee, and "the heads of other relevant Federal agencies, and the commercial space sector". These reports will clarify how commercial space launches will be authorized and supervised (Sec. 108), the management of space traffic and space assets of both the government and private sectors (Sec 109), and releasing "safety-related space situational awareness data" in a manner consistent with national security concerns (Sec. 110). Section 111 focuses on developing "regulatory approaches" and "performance standards" for the commercial sector, requiring ongoing reports through 2021 on "the progress of the commercial space transportation industry in developing voluntary industry consensus standards that promote best practices to improve industry safety" and a report "specifying key industry metrics that might indicate readiness of the commercial space sector" to adopt a "safety framework" as mandated.

NOAA Commercial Space Policy. H.R. 2262 Title III addresses the role of the Office of Space Commerce after renaming it from the Office of Space Commercialization. This agency operates under the National Oceanic and Atmospheric Administration (NOAA), which in turn operates under the U.S. Department of Commerce. In January 2016, less than two months after the enactment of H.R. 2262, the NOAA issued its Commercial Space Policy. This policy designates the Office of Space Commerce "as a single point of entry for commercial providers" to work with the agency on its data collection, its promotion of the space industry, and improving its mission capabilities (NOAA, Jan. 2016). On March 16, 2016, NOAA took another step to "provide transparency to the commercial industry" by posting its satellite requirements, including requirements for the Deep Space Climate Observatory (DSCOVR) which "had not previously been available to the public" (NOAA, Mar 2016).

Space Mineral Resources draws attention to a policy "vacuum" of legal frameworks and property rights for asteroid mining, an industry the authors describe as "embryonic". However, within months of its publication, H.R. 2262 has taken the first steps to address this policy vacuum and create a policy regime to stimulate commercial industry involvement. As the NOAA continues to integrate the commercial sector into its agency goals, and as the reports from the Secretary of Transportation and the President come in this year, we will see definitive progress towards policy that fosters public-private cooperation in exploring space and extracting its resources. And, by recognizing its existing treaty obligations, H.R. 2262 models how a nation might create its own unique responses to the industry while remaining a team player on the international level.

Luxembourg. The U.S. is not the only country interested in defining extraterrestrial property rights through public policy. In February 2016 the Luxembourg Ministry of the Economy announced a similar policy initiative. "Luxembourg is the first European country to announce its intention to set out a formal legal framework which ensures that private operators working in space can be confident about their rights to the resources they extract, i.e. rare minerals from asteroids" (Luxembourg, 2016). As an example of the economic significance of public-private partnerships in this new industry, the Ministry says it will "consider direct capital investment in companies active in this field" (ibid). Luxembourg is preparing this policy as part of their SpaceResources.lu budget, which will fit into the international framework of "the next multiannual budget of the European Space Agency, to be decided in December 2016" (ibid).

To date, "Luxembourg and the U.S. are the only two countries in the world who have begun to take legal action toward securing property rights for commercial companies who could, one day, collect rare and precious resources from asteroids" (Orwig, 2016). But it seems likely that other nations will begin to follow suit as excitement about the economic possibilities of asteroid mining continues to rise. "National laws are the major framework that individual actors, both private and government, will accept as a means for specifically developing and acting in space," write the authors of *Space Mineral Resources*, but "international law will be the most relevant to prevent and solve potential international conflicts of interest concerning space actors from different countries" (Dula, 2015). National policy will need to be consistent with international law to create legal certainty and clarity for the asteroid mining industry. The near future should prove whether the policies from the U.S. and Luxembourg will serve as models for other nations, or if we will see different approaches to extraterrestrial property rights.

Part Two: Economics and Cooperation between Public and Private Sectors.

If the main goal is economic stimulation, then what will make asteroid mining economically viable? Dante Lauretta of the University of Tucson, principal investigator for NASA's OSIRIS-REx mission to the asteroid Bennu, points out the economic challenge inherent in asteroid mining. Laurette estimates that "for the recoverable value in any given asteroid, you're spending half that to bring it back" to Earth (Science Teacher, 2013, p. 16). This idea that mined asteroid resources will be brought to Earth may represent the popular conception of asteroid mining. After all, what is the point of mining in space if we do not bring the materials to Earth? But, the massive cost of doing so has prompted researchers to argue the best economic use is to keep them in space.

V. The Case for a Space-Based Market.

In *Asteroid Mining 101*, John S. Lewis creates a case for a space-based economy as a necessity for successful exploitation of asteroid resources. Its proposals include using water—and other elements currently found as ice in asteroids—for propellants (rocket fuel), and using mined ferrous metals for constructing equipment and dwellings in space. The authors of *Space Mineral Resources* agree that a mining industry "based upon precious metals to terrestrial markets alone appears to be a non-starter", and that making asteroid mining economically feasible would depend on having "in-space customers for propellants, consumables, structural materials, and shielding" (Dula, 2015).

The Influence of Gravity. Earth's gravity is largely to blame for this dim view of bringing extracted resources to Earth. Put simply, it requires a huge and expensive amount of fuel to launch a rocket from Earth's surface and propel it through the atmosphere into space. And by comparison, it takes miniscule amounts of fuel to move a vessel through space outside of Earth's sphere of gravitational influence and in a vacuum or near-vacuum. Mathematically speaking, the important figure in calculating the energy of getting a spacecraft from one point to another is expressed in the term "delta V", meaning the required change in velocity, with the necessary energy being proportional to the square of delta V (Lewis, 2015, p. 82).

In terms of delta V, the Moon is less accessible than Mars' moons and the estimated 3800 Near Earth Asteroids (NEAs) because of the high delta V required to both land a spacecraft on the Moon safely and to relaunch that craft from it (ibid, p. 84). Ten years ago, in a paper published in the *AIP Conference Proceedings*, Ken Erickson predicted several things as "reasonably likely" to be "realized or about to be put in place" by 2015: "substantial orbital tourism, tourist trips to the Moon, human exploration of the lunar surface for scientific and economic purposes, and robotic and human scouting missions with intention of building lunar bases" (Erickson, 2006, p. 1150). He based the likelihood of these events on "lunar exploration initiatives of the U.S., Russia, E.U., China, and others", as well as the expected increase in demand for certain resources (ibid, 2006, p. 1148).

But these things have not come to pass to any significant degree, and the Moon's gravitational strength is a major reason why they have not. Near Earth asteroids now seem a much more likely target for resource extraction, considering their high resource potential and the low delta V required to exploit it. A space-based economy with construction and launches from low Earth orbit to and from NEAs would greatly reduce the incredible cost of propellants needed to overcome gravity.

Using Resources in Space. John S. Lewis identifies "an in-space demand for ferrous metals" as a condition for the economic viability of extracting platinum-group metals (PGMs) from asteroids (Lewis, 2015, p. 113). PGMs will not be mined directly, but are "lucrative byproducts" of mining ferrous metals, such as iron and nickel (ibid, p. 109-10). Space-based construction would use ferrous metals to build equipment, satellites, housing, research stations, probes, and other tools of exploration. Lewis also applies this space-based approach to resources which could serve as propellants. Water mined from asteroids and extinct comets which now orbit like asteroids could be used in steam-based propulsion systems, such as those that heat water using refracted sun rays (solar thermal propulsion) and those that run water over a nuclear reactor core to make steam (nuclear thermal propulsion) (ibid, p. 107).

Space Mineral Resources calls water "the currency of space" and sees the establishment of spaceports "selling water that was mined from the Moon or asteroids" as a necessity for expanding human activities beyond Earth (Dula, 2015). Water will play an important role in generating energy, serving as propellant, enabling extraterrestrial agriculture, and, of course, fulfilling humans' biological need to drink it (ibid). Water is also an effective radiation shield, even more effective than the silicates found in many asteroids, and could be incorporated into the architecture of spacecraft and moveable housing to protect humans from damage by cosmic radiation (Lewis, 2015, p. 102, 108-9). Earth's atmosphere protects humans on this planet, but radiation exposure in space presents a serious threat. Therefore, despite the popular notion of mining asteroids to make a fortune in rare metals, water may well prove to be the most important resource extracted from celestial bodies.

These conclusions bring to light the kinds of industries and technological innovations the President and federal agencies will need to "encourage" per H.R. 2262, Title IV. Federal policy makers will need to think beyond the limited and economically flawed idea of bringing resources to Earth, and instead focus on creating the space-based market that will make the best use of those resources.

VI. The Risk of Price Crashes and Other Economic Considerations.

Price Crashes in Mineral Markets. The literature advocating asteroid mining often touts the monetary value of asteroid-bound minerals as a major incentive for developing the industry. But this value creates a problem which public policy may need to solve: the risk of a price crash that would utterly devalue said minerals. *Asteroid Mining 101* offers the following estimates of minerals present in the Near Earth Asteroids (NEAs), not to be confused with the Asteroid Belt between Mars and Jupiter.

"Given the total mass of the NEA swarm of 120×10^{15} kg, it is possible to calculate the Earth-surface market value of its materials at present market prices. The balance sheet includes 37×10^{15} kg of iron worth \$11,000 trillion, 2.5×10^9 kg of Ni [nickel] worth \$70,000 trillion, 2×10^8 kg of cobalt worth another \$70,000 trillion, and 1.8×10^6 kg of PGMs [platinum group metals] worth yet another $70,000 trillion" (Lewis, 2015, p. 113).

Although Lewis believes "there is absolutely no prospect of importing even a tiny proportion of these materials to Earth", he cautions that importing PGMs to Earth only makes economic sense "if the PGM import rate is tightly controlled so as to avoid a price crash" (ibid). Flooding Earth's market with rare resources would drive their prices down, inadvertently de-incentivizing a mining operation, from an economic standpoint. As *The Independent Review's* write-up on *Asteroid Mining 101* states, Lewis' estimated monetary value of asteroid ores "should not be taken literally—bringing these ores to market would obviously greatly decrease their price due to the massive supply increase" (Salter, p. 459). Currently, no public policy addresses this risk of a price crash, perhaps because even NASA's ambitious OSIRIS-REx mission only aims to bring back 60 grams of asteroid samples from its seven-year mission to Bennu and back (NASA, Feb. 2016). But as technology develops over the next few years and science fiction begins to turn into science fact, policy makers will undoubtedly need to address price control and market regulation.

Insurance and Licensing. Title I of H.R. 2262 addresses two other economic concerns for the budding commercial space exploration industry: insurance claims and licensing. Section 102 charges the Secretary of Transportation to evaluate and, if necessary, update the "methodology used to calculate the maximum probable loss under section 50914 of Title 51, United States Code". This section of the U.S. Code concerns "liability insurance and financial responsibility requirements" related to any death, injury, or property damages caused by space launches and re-entries. It requires an annual report every May 15, and—as amended by the Act—gives federal courts the exclusive jurisdiction over claims. H.R. 2262 mandates the Comptroller General to evaluate and report on the results of the report, and any steps required to implement it.

Section 105 requires the Secretary of Transportation to submit a report "on approaches for streamlining the licensing and permitting process of launch vehicles, reentry vehicles" and their components to "improve efficiency, reduce unnecessary costs, resolve inconsistencies, remove duplication, and minimize unwarranted constraints" as well as assess "existing private and government infrastructure... in future licensing activities". Clearly the federal government wants to make sure companies are not only properly insured but properly licensed for the protection of all those involved, and to clarify the process to achieve these goals.

VII. Uniting the Public and Private Sectors.

Arguments for Private-Sector Leadership. The much-publicized increase in private space launches parallels a shift towards an attitude Ken Erickson describes as, "Yes, people do go into space on their own, recreationally, without needing a huge government agency to do it" (Erickson, 2006, p. 1151). In keeping with this private-not-public approach to space exploration and mining, Erickson's *Next X-Prize* article sets forth a detailed program in which private industry would offer a cash prize in a competition to establish a viable base at L1, one of the five Lagrange points where, due to the physics of gravity, an object could maintain a stable position in space relative to the Earth and Moon. Erickson models this proposal on "the Ansari X-prize that led to the first private manned flight into space by Scaled Composites" (Erickson, 2007, p. 1145). He cites The Aldridge Commission's 2004 report that estimated this $10 million prize created a "$400 million private and industry investment supporting the many teams competing to win the prize", effectively creating a demand and resulting in economic stimulation.

A principal finding of the study presented in *Space Mineral Resources* also supports this idea of private enterprise operating independently from the government.

"SMR ventures cannot wait for government programs to lower technological and programmatic risks. Commercial ventures must determine the optimum path for commercial success and aggressively lead the way beyond low Earth orbit (LEO). During the first half of the 21st century, space leadership will come from commercial enterprises and not depend upon government space programs" (Dula, 2015).

The authors of this study suggest that commercial enterprises will get to space first and "will be able to support government explorations by selling products to them" at designated locations (ibid). The study took place under the auspices of the International Academy of Astronautics (IAA), a non-governmental organization, and several commercial firms contributed to it: Moon Express, Excalibur Exploration Limited, Deep Space Industries (also the publisher of *Asteroid Mining 101*), Ad Astra Rocket Company, and Shackleton Energy Company. One might expect publications involving commercial space exploration companies to be somewhat biased in favor of private-sector leadership.

These arguments for private-sector leadership in asteroid mining may appeal to those who see government-led exploration as little more than a sinkhole for tax dollars. Erickson criticizes the International Space Station (ISS) as a "government enterprise" which has "stagnated" and "consumed the scientific, technical, and creative energies of many nations, without repaying them a dollar" (Erickson, 2007, p. 1146).

As if in answer to these criticisms, H.R. 2262 addresses the economics of the International Space Station. First, H.R. 2262 Title I Section 114 amends The NASA Act of 2010 to extend the U.S. commitment to using and maintaining the ISS to 2024, from the previous date of 2020. NASA is directed to "pursue international, commercial, and intragovernmental means to maximize ISS logistics supply, maintenance, and operational capabilities, reduce risks to ISS systems sustainability, and offset and minimize United States operations costs relating to the ISS" (42 U.S.C, § 18351). H.R. 2262 states the importance of ensuring "the greatest return on investments made by the United States and its international partners in the development, assembly, and operations" of the ISS, and the importance of taking "all necessary steps" to keep the ISS "viable and productive" in support of "exploration and partnership strategies". This language makes it clear that Congress views the ISS not as a financial liability but a facility that can support commercial partnerships that make money, not lose it.

Arguments for private-sector leadership sometimes gloss over the fact that even private companies use government infrastructure. For example, the commercial company SpaceX uses launch pad 39A at Kennedy Space Center in Cape Canaveral, Florida under a 20-year agreement signed in 2014 with NASA (NASA, 2014). This is the same launch site used for, among other historic events, the launching of Apollo 11 for the first manned Moon landing in 1969 (ibid). The Center's Director, Bob Cabana, sees repurposing such historic facilities as part of a "plan for a multi-user spaceport shared by government and commercial partners" (ibid). And despite his criticisms, Erickson argues his proposed L1 base would involve "private industry, government agencies, and wealthy entrepreneurs", all of whom "stand to gain" from the endeavor (Erickson, 2007, p. 1146). While the private sector takes an increasingly prominent role in exploring space and the quest to extract its resources, the result is not a private-versus-public scenario. Instead, government policy such as H.R. 2262 provides the legal framework, government infrastructure provides the technological foundation for private enterprise, and the result is collaboration and cooperation.

NASA and Public-Private Collaboration. NASA's research and pioneering efforts pave the way for the private sector and its partnerships with public agencies. Two NASA missions exemplify their leadership and partnerships. First, NASA remains a leader in the study of the Asteroid Belt between Mars and Jupiter, having recently given the world its most detailed study of 4 Vesta, the second-largest known asteroid in the Belt. NASA's Dawn Mission began its interplanetary cruise in December 2007, settling into its first orbit around the asteroid Vesta in July, 2011. Its measurements gave "scientists a near 3-D view into Vesta's internal structure", "obtained the highest-resolution surface temperature maps of any asteroid visited by a spacecraft", and revealed new information about the asteroid's surface features and mineral content (Cook, 2012). The Dawn spacecraft next moved to the largest-known Belt asteroid, Ceres, entering into its orbit in 2015, and continuing to send back images and data to Earth at the time of this writing. (Dates for the Dawn Mission come from the Mission Status Updates by Chief Engineer/Mission Director Marc Rayman.)

NASA's leadership in asteroid exploration includes studies of the Near Earth Asteroids, too. NASA has scheduled its spacecraft OSIRIS-REx to launch in September 2016, with an anticipated return date in 2023. OSIRIS-REx stands for "Origins, Spectral Interpretation, Resource Identification, Security-Regolith Explorer". Dante Lauretta of the University of Tucson, principal investigator the mission, describes it as a "proof of concept" which will "develop important technologies for asteroid exploration that will benefit anyone interested in exploring or mining asteroids, whether it's NASA or a private company" (Science Teacher, 2013, p. 14). It will be the "first U.S. mission to collect a sample of an asteroid and return it to Earth for study" (NASA, Feb. 2016). The governmental sector is clearly providing leadership. But did NASA build the spacecraft? No. That job fell to "Lockheed Martin Space Systems in Denver", a division of the prominent defense contractor Lockheed Martin (ibid). There is no reason to draw a line between government and commercial contributions to these efforts. Rather, partnerships between public and private agencies make them possible.

The Academic Sector. The role of public universities in these endeavors is exemplified by the student-designed equipment included in the OSIRIS-REx mission. "The Regolith X-ray Imaging Spectrometer (REXIS) will determine elemental abundances on the surface of asteroid Bennu, complementing the mineral and chemical mapping capabilities provided by two other instruments on the spacecraft" (NASA, Jan. 2016). This REXIS instrument is essentially a telescope that will image the fluorescence of the regolith on the asteroid's surface as solar x-rays interact with it, "allowing the production of maps of the different elements present on Bennu's surface" (ibid). Students working with faculty designed the instrument, and more than 100 students from MIT and Harvard will be involved in the mission, performing "data analysis as part of their coursework" (ibid). The OSIRIS-REx mission demonstrates the important role the public sector plays in forming collaborative partnerships. By drawing on the intellectual capital of universities, NASA missions engage institutions from the academic sector.

Members of the academic community also serve in advisory roles, such as Dante Lauretta, quoted above, and *Asteroid Mining 101* author John S. Lewis, who served as an advisor to NASA numerous times. Arizona State University boasts a Mars Space Flight Facility which has contributed to recent Mars missions such as NASA's Mars Science Laboratory, a rover spacecraft whose landing site was chosen using data from ASU's Thermal Emission Imaging System (THEMIS) aboard NASA's orbiting Mars Odyssey spacecraft. The academic sector plays an increasingly important and publicly recognized role in furthering space exploration.

But universities also stand to gain financially from intellectual property rights to the technologies they develop. U.S. law grants universities ownership of the technologies and inventions developed by students and faculty using university resources (Ferrera, 2012, p. 40). The Bayh-Doyle Act of 1980 enabled universities to take title to inventions developed in the course of federally-sponsored work, resulting in thousands of commercial product launches and billions of dollars in revenue for universities (ibid, p. 41). Universities often retain these rights and then license them to students who commercialize them, with Stanford University's patent ownership of Google's underlying PageRank algorithm being but one famous example (ibid, p. 41-2).

Conversely, NASA's Technology Transfer Program works to bring its own patented technologies to business students who may develop commercial business plans around licensing NASA's tech. In one successful example of this collaborative effort, a student-faculty team at Rollins College developed a prototype and commercialization plan to bring to market a sensor developed by NASA (Heiney, 2012). According to NASA's Technology Transfer University, this sensor was "originally developed to inspect windows on the space shuttle" (T2U).

Therefore, we can expect to see universities becoming an important economic force in the future of asteroid mining, as they will hold the intellectual property rights to the innovations they contribute to these joint efforts between the public and private sectors, and have opportunities to work with NASA on commercializing existing technologies. The future of space exploration and asteroid mining promises to be a significant source of economic and educational opportunities for universities.

VIII. Conclusion.

In an editorial piece in 2000 entitled *The Shape of Kleopatra*, *Science* magazine editor William K. Hartmann wrote,
> "The idea of asteroid mining raises the question of who owns the resources. Is there a social mechanism by which the benefit of such resources can be spread to all humanity, instead of increasing sociopolitical instability by making only the discoverers (or discovering nations) rich and increasing the gap between the first and third worlds?"

Now, sixteen years later, The U.S. Commercial Space Launch Competitiveness Act has given the world its first clear public policy concerning property rights to resources extracted from asteroids and other celestial objects. It has also spurred the development of new policies concerning safety regulations, launch coordination, and partnerships between the governmental and commercial sectors. These will become clear by the end of 2016, both in offices of the U.S. government and in other countries. But as the possibilities for the industry congeal into new realities, Hartmann's question remains unanswered. Will the potentially vast wealth of space-based resources benefit all humanity, or will it be concentrated in the hands of the already wealthy who can afford the massive expenses to explore, extract, and claim it? If profit motives and competition have vanquished the idea of space resources being the "common heritage of mankind" in international and national law, then we must hope the resultant economic stimulation from the commercial asteroid mining industry will benefit societies as a whole by strengthening the public, private, and academic sectors. The resources of space await humanity and draw ever closer to our technological grasp. It will be up to us to use them wisely.

References

Agreement Governing the Activities of States on the Moon and Other Celestial Bodies (The Moon Treaty). (1979). http://disarmament.un.org/treaties/t/moon/text

Arizona State University (ASU). "THEMIS Support for MSL." *Mars Space Flight Facility.* https://themis.asu.edu/landingsites

Babin, Brian. (9 December, 2015). *Remarks to the 10th Eilene Galloway Symposium on Critical Issues in Space Law.* http://pri.wpengine.netdna-cdn.com/wp-content/uploads/2015/12/2015-12-9-Galloway-Speech-for-CBB.pdf

Brooks, Michael. (21 February, 2014). "Lunar land-grab." *New Statesman, 143*(5198): 24-27.

"Can We Mine Asteroids?" (October, 2013). *Science Teacher, 80*(7): 14-16.

Code of Laws of the United States of America. 42 U.S.C. § 18351 https://www.law.cornell.edu/uscode/text/42/18351 51 U.S.C. § 50902 https://www.law.cornell.edu/uscode/text/51/50902 51 U.S.C. § 50914 https://www.law.cornell.edu/uscode/text/51/50914

Cook, Jia-Rui C. (25 April, 2012). "Dawn Reveals Secrets of Giant Asteroid Vesta" (News Release). *Jet Propulsion Laboratory,* California Institute of Technology. http://dawn.jpl.nasa.gov/news/asteroid_vesta_secrets_reveale d.asp

Dula, Arthur, and Zhenjun, Zhang, Editors. (27 November, 2015). *Space Mineral Resources: A Global Assessment of the*

Challenges and Opportunities. Virginia Edition Publishing Company.

Encyclopædia Britannica. (2014). "Sovereignty." http://www.britannica.com/topic/sovereignty

Erickson, Ken R. (2006). "Next X-Prize: L1 Base with Linked Asteroid Mining as Prime Catalyst for Space Enterprise." *AIP Conference Proceedings, 813*(1): 1145-1152. DOI: 10.1063/1.2169296

Erickson, Ken R. (2007). "Optimal Architecture for an Asteroid Mining Mission: System Components and Project Execution." *AIP Conference Proceedings, 880*(1): 896-903. DOI: 10.1063/1.2437531

Ferrera, Gerald R., et. al. (2012). *CyberLaw Text & Cases (Third Edition)*. Mason, OH: South-Western, Cengage Learning.

Hartmann, William K. (2000). "The Shape of Kleopatra." *Science, 288*(5467).

Heiney, Anna. (12 December, 2012). "Business Students Accelerate NASA Technologies to Market". *NASA John F. Kennedy Space Center*. http://www.nasa.gov/centers/kennedy/news/nasa_rollins.html

H.R. 2262: The US Commercial Space Launch Competitiveness Act. https://www.congress.gov/bill/114th-congress/house-bill/2262/text

Lewis, John S. (2015). *Asteroid Mining 101: Wealth for the New Space Economy*. Deep Space Industries, Inc.

Luxembourg Ministry of the Economy. (2 February, 2016). "Luxembourg to launch framework to support the future use

of space resources." *Government.lu.*
http://www.gouvernement.lu/5653386

National Aeronautics and Space Administration (NASA). (7 January, 2016). "Student-Built Experiment Integrated onto NASA's OSIRIS-REx Mission." *NASA Status Report.* http://www.nasa.gov/press-release/goddard/2016/student-built-experiment-integrated-onto-nasa-s-osiris-rex-mission

NASA. (19 February, 2016). "NASA Invites Public to Send Artwork to an Asteroid." *NASA Press Release.* https://www.nasa.gov/press-release/nasa-invites-public-to-send-artwork-to-an-asteroid

NASA. (15 April, 2014). "NASA Signs Agreement with SpaceX for Use of Historic Launch Pad." *NASA Press Release.* https://www.nasa.gov/press/2014/april/nasa-signs-agreement-with-spacex-for-use-of-historic-launch-pad/#.VvF-zzEvfl8

National Oceanic and Atmospheric Administration (NOAA). (8 January, 2016). "NOAA Issues Commercial Space Policy." http://www.space.commerce.gov/noaa-issues-commercial-space-policy/ and http://www.noaanews.noaa.gov/stories2016/010816-noaa-statement-commercial-space-policy.html

NOAA. (16 March, 2016). "NOAA Satellite Program Requirements Posted." http://www.space.commerce.gov/noaa-satellite-program-requirements-posted/

Orwig, Jessica. (5 February, 2016). "A tiny European country just made an unprecedented move in the space mining business." *Business Insider.* http://www.businessinsider.com/luxembourg-wants-to-cash-in-on-asteroid-mining-2016-2

Planetary Resources. (9 December, 2015). "Representative Brian Babin Speaks about Space Law at the Galloway Symposium." http://www.planetaryresources.com/2015/12/representative-brian-babin-speaks-about-space-law-at-the-galloway-symposium/

Rayman, Marc. (2007, 2011, 2015, 2016). "Mission Status Updates" (Dawn). *Jet Propulsion Laboratory*, California Institute of Technology. http://dawn.jpl.nasa.gov/mission/status.html

Riederer, Rachel. (Fall, 2014). "Whose Moon is It Anyway?" *Dissent*, 61(4): 6-10.

Salter, Alexander William. (Winter, 2016). Untitled Review of Asteroid Mining 101: Wealth for the New Space Economy. *The Independent Review*, 20(3): 458-460.

Technology Transfer University (T2U). "Bringing NASA Technology into the Classroom." *NASA Technology Transfer Program*. http://technology.nasa.gov/t2u

Treaty on Principles Governing the Activities of States in the Exploration and Use of Outer Space, including the Moon and Other Celestial Bodies (The Outer Space Treaty). (1967). http://disarmament.un.org/treaties/t/outer_space/text

3

Net Neutrality for Broadband:
Understanding the FCC's 2015 Open Internet Order

Abstract

Annotated Bibliography

Abstract

The FCC's 2015 Open Internet Order reclassified high-speed broadband Internet access as a telecommunications service subject to common carriage requirements under Title II of the Telecommunications Act of 1996 following decades of technological convergence, litigation, and increasing popular and political pressure. The Order's service requirements and ban on paid prioritization, though contentious, pave the way for the FCC's vision of nationwide broadband. As beneficial as the net neutrality rules may be, the FCC's legal battles are far from over.

Keywords: Federal Communications Commission, FCC, 2015 Open Internet Order, telecommunications, Internet, broadband, public policy, net neutrality, regulation, Title II

I. Introduction.

The Federal Communications Commission's 2015 Open Internet Order, championed as a major advance in establishing net neutrality, reclassifies broadband Internet access as a common carriage telecommunication service rather than an information service. The agency's new classification brings broadband under the Title II authority of the Telecommunications Act of 1996. Why is this such an important move for the FCC?

To begin with, the Telecommunications Act of 1996 did not foresee technologies converging. It failed to anticipate that future emerging technologies would bring competing services onto different physical networks than the ones traditionally associated with them. This resulted in numerous, lengthy court cases where judges had to puzzle over such questions as whether the FCC has Title VI authority to regulate streaming video over the internet like it does with multichannel video programming, or if the FCC has Title II authority to regulate Voice over IP services on broadband like it does with traditional wireline telephony. Or, does any service provided over the Internet fall under the incredibly vague authority given in Title I? Lawyers argued these points for years, but nobody knew for sure, and consensus was hard to come by.

With such matters tied up in the courts, it is no wonder that regulation had completely failed to keep up with the engineering realities of Internet technology. The new Title II classification of broadband as a telecommunications service has the potential to eliminate this litigious waste of time and resources by clearly defining the FCC's authority and allowing the agency to move forward. The reclassification also brings regulatory authority into a more realistic alignment with technology. Just as technology has converged, regulation is converging. Rather than having all these services spread out into separate Titles, they now converge into one: Title II.

Though the reclassification rode a wave of popular and political support, it is not without its detractors. The 2015 Open Internet Order, opposed by many corporate interests in the

Internet industry, faces potential legislative and judicial challenges. In seeking to resolve longstanding questions, the Order brings its own battery of economic and engineering difficulties in a time when the FCC seeks to promote expansion of broadband nationwide, even into traditionally underserved and rural communities. This essay will affirm the FCC's decision and its intended benefits, summarize the technological and legal background leading up to it, and highlight the significant political and technological challenges which remain to be solved.

II. Technological Background of Classifying Broadband.

The technical aspects summarized in this section receive a more detailed, historical analysis in the book *Digital Crossroads: Telecommunications Law and Policy in the Internet Age* by Jonathan E. Nuechterlein and Philip J. Weiser, especially chapters 1, 2 and 5. (See the Annotated Bibliography.)

From Waves to Digits. The problem of regulating Internet access, and the question of the FCC's scope of authority in doing so, began with the technology that made it all possible: digital encoding of information. When information began to go digital, telecommunication was an analog industry. From vinyl records to telephone signals, communication relied on creating physical and electrical analogs of sound waves (or, as in photography and other visual media, light waves). From the physical grooves in a vinyl record to the electromagnetic waves which power speakers and amplifiers, information was re-created in a physical form analogous to the information source.

Digital technology changed all that. Digital technology sampled the information source, numerous times per second, and broke that sample down into a binary code: a string of ones and zeroes. The two binary digits communicated a state to transistors: on or off, open or closed. Transmitting these digital samples created the world of packets, where the encoded information would be broken down into smaller pieces. Each packet contained additional code which identified what larger group it belonged to, and where it belonged in the sequence of samples. The signal's receiver would reassemble all the packets in the correct order according to this additional information in the packet headers.

A Binary Journey. This method came with certain challenges for transmitting information "live" or in "real time". The receiver might put the packets together out of order, a phenomenon known as jitter. Or, it might take different packets different lengths of time to arrive at the receiver, creating a waiting period known as latency (or, more commonly, "lag"). Advances in digital technology eventually solved much of these problems. However, they are important to keep in mind when understanding some of the arguments against net neutrality and the 2015 Open Internet Order.

To ensure that packets would not take too long to travel from transmitter to receiver, Internet networks and service or content providers developed paid prioritization. For example, a provider of videoconferencing services would want to avoid latency and delays in the signals for a conference, wanting instead for the users to have a smooth, uninterrupted service. So, the provider would pay the networks to prioritize the relevant packets. It seemed like a good solution, and still does to a great number of companies in the digital information industry. After all, packets conveying an email message or a text-only web page do not need to be constantly transmitted "live". Those can be sent one time, and super-fast speed is not so important to the user's receipt and enjoyment of the signal. Paid prioritization became a way for providers to ensure a reasonably high quality of service for urgent signals, and for networks to have a financial incentive to make that possible. The FCC's declaring an end to these paid prioritization agreements remains a contentious aspect of the 2015 Open Internet Order.

The Rise of Cable and Dial-up. The Order's reclassifying Internet access as a telecommunications service has also garnered many objections. So, it helps to understand the technological background underlying this dispute. Broadband Internet access, though now possible through both physical cables and wireless radio waves, began with the rise of cable television. Cable TV companies competed with the older television networks by building a massive infrastructure to run coaxial cable directly to people's residences. This robust cable network could provide more bandwidth and a more reliable signal than the existing radio wave networks. Eventually, these cable companies began to maximize those advantages by offering Internet access, too.

But before that happened, Internet access took place using the existing infrastructure of the telephone companies. To access the Internet, a user connected a computer modem to a phone line and dialed up an Internet service provider on the same network they would use to place a phone call. This dial-up technology gave rise to one of the fundamental problems of definition that has plagued regulators for roughly twenty years.

The Convergence. The FCC had developed regulatory approaches to the existing copper-wire telephone networks, and telephony was seen as a distinctly different service than the digital information service provided by the Internet. Telecommunications generally meant telephone service, and its regulation focused on restraining the monopolistic power of the phone companies: first, AT&T with its massive nationwide network which enabled long-distance calls, and later the Bell companies formed by splitting up AT&T into smaller companies which provided primarily local telephone service. Because the Internet spawned the birth of companies not related to AT&T and the Bells, and because its digital data processing capabilities bore little resemblance to analog phone service, the FCC saw telephony and Internet as two very separate things.

However, one can easily see the problem of treating Internet access differently when it is accessed using the very same physical infrastructure as telephone service thanks to dial-up technology. As technologies began to converge, "telephone" calls became possible over the new digital and cable networks. Treating these services differently became increasingly problematic. The Internet eventually made it possible to use the same infrastructure and networks to access data processing and information services, participate in voice communication, receive video content and music, and any form of information which could be digitally sampled and encoded. Technology had at last converged. But, as we shall see, regulation experienced its own difficult form of latency, lagging far behind this technological convergence. The problems thus created are problems the 2015 Open Internet Order seeks to resolve.

III. Legal Background of Classifying Broadband.

The Telecommunications Act of 1996. In 1996, Congress updated an Act from 1934, the same Act which created the FCC and laid the foundation for the agency's authority. At that time, the FCC's major concerns included encouraging the interstate telephone network to become a truly universal service for all citizens, not simply by expanding networks but by keeping prices for residential customers low (Nuechterlein, 2013, p. 38). The FCC focused on encouraging competition in the telecommunications industry by removing barriers to entry for new companies (ibid, p. 52). As part of achieving these goals, the FCC required nondiscrimination in both pricing and services. A telephone company could charge for its service or charge to lease its network capacity and facilities. But, it could not give preferential pricing to different parties for those things.

The FCC's authority to make these requirements came from certain sections of the Communications Act known together as Title II (Jacobs, 2015, p. 1). Title II set forth the FCC's scope of powers to regulate telephony as a common carriage service (Nuechterlein, 2013, p. 21). "Generally, common carriage refers to a requirement that all customers be offered service on a standardized and non-discriminatory basis, and may include a requirement that those services be priced reasonably" (Ruane, 2014, p. 12).

But by 1996, new technologies had arrived, including the Internet. The updated Act distinguished between traditional telephony (a telecommunications service) and information services, placing the latter not under Title II but under Title I

(Signaigo, 2007, p. 2). Title I did not have the same common carriage aspects as Title II (ibid). In fact, Title I gave the FCC "little specific jurisdictional guidance" (Ohlhausen, 2015, p. 208). With its authority to regulate Title I information services so vaguely defined, the FCC invoked a similarly vague "ancillary authority" in this area (Nuechterlein, 2013, p. 232). This unfortunate state of affairs resulted in much debate in the courts when the FCC attempted to regulate information services, including Internet access.

But the Title I classification of Internet access had more problems than ill-defined regulatory authority. It also suffered from an acute lack of foresight into the Internet's emerging technology. It failed to foresee a world where convergence would blur the distinctions between telecommunications and the types of data processing which fell under the information services classification (ibid, p. 231). The 1996 Act, coming into effect just as email, web sites, and search engines were becoming fully integrated into daily life, quickly became obsolete in its treatment of Internet regulation. Splitting voice, video, and information into separate Titles began to make little sense. "With the convergence of various technologies—for instance, Voice over Internet Protocol (VoIP) competing with circuit-switched telephony or Internet Protocol Television (IPTV) competing with broadcast and cable—this siloed approach to regulation is increasingly out of step with reality" (Ohlhausen, 2015, p. 208). The difference between the various Titles rapidly became more and more irrelevant to a world where voice, video, audio, and text could all be digitally encoded and served over the Internet.

The Judicial Battleground. In the wake of this sorely flawed legislation, the FCC's attempts to regulate aspects of the Internet typically met with litigation. Federal courts would be asked to interpret the scope of the FCC's authority based on the law as provided by the Act. Was a regulatory measure within the FCC's scope of power? Had the FCC correctly interpreted the classification of telecommunication service versus information service? Was the agency's regulation allowable under Title I or Title II? Just what does "ancillary authority" mean?

These questions required judges to sort through incredibly complex engineering and economic arguments which would have more easily been settled by clear and realistic legislative guidelines. But with only the inadequate wording of the 1996 Act to guide them, judges found themselves struggling to craft logical and meaningful interpretations. They also found themselves in disagreement, as differences of opinion between State, Circuit, and the Supreme Courts revealed, as well as the number of dissenting opinions which revealed a lack of consensus about these matters even within a single court. In short, "the legislature, the courts, and the FCC have all grappled with definitions, and the results have been generally confusing and inconsistent" (Signaigo, 2007, p. 1). At the heart of many of these judicial battles lay the question of whether or not the Internet was a telecommunication service or an information service, and therefore if it would fall under Title II or Title I, respectively. This debate came to a head in the *Brand X* case.

The *Brand X* Decision. A simplistic understanding of *Brand X* would lead one to believe the Supreme Court had ruled broadband Internet access was an information service, in agreement with the FCC's classification at that time. However, the Supreme Court opinion merely recognizes this classification was a *reasonable* interpretation on the FCC's part, even if it was not the *best* or *only* interpretation. The opinion argues that, due to the vague wording of the 1996 Act, it is entirely within the FCC's authority as a federal agency to make its own reasonable interpretation.

> "If a statute is ambiguous, and if the implementing agency's construction is reasonable, *Chevron* requires a federal court to accept the agency's construction of the statute, even if the agency's reading differs from what the court believes is the best statutory interpretation" (p. 8).

The majority opinion found the classification reasonable, but the dissenting opinion by Justice Scalia expresses animosity towards it. The majority accepted arguments that the telecommunications hardware involved was an inseparable part of the tools to access the service, a service which could be understood as information service. Therefore, the majority reasoned, the hardware did not necessarily change the underlying nature of the service. Scalia's dissent argued against this reasoning, asserting that the use of telecommunications hardware was an obvious use of telecommunication service, and that divorcing the service and the access network into two types of classifications made no practical sense. This dissent agreed with the lower court which had decided that broadband access was clearly a telecommunication service and could not legitimately be regulated as anything but. The majority handled this logic by making it clear it was not up to the courts to decide the classification, per the *Chevron* precedence. It was, in the majority's opinion, the responsibility of the FCC to make the classification, and courts should uphold the FCC decision even if they did not agree with it, as long as the decision was reasonable.

This case makes two things clear. First, the courts have a major problem finding consensus on a law that arbitrarily splits telecommunication and information into two different things. It is a split which defies logic and therefore makes logical, consistent conclusions nearly impossible. As one analysis of the Brand X case summarizes it,

> "The difficulty that the FCC and the courts have had with shoehorning modern technologies into the FCC classifications simply underscores the need for change or even elimination of these classifications. Distinguishing between 'basic' telecommunications service and 'enhanced' information services no longer makes sense in light of the complexity of these technologies" (Signaigo, 2007, p. 395).

Second, the responsibility and authority to choose how the Internet is classified rests not with the courts but with the FCC. The *Brand X* decision holds that the FCC may, under current law, decide whether or not broadband Internet is a telecommunication service or an information service. The FCC's interpretation of *Brand X* agrees with this analysis. As Section C.43 of the 2015 Order puts it,

"Exercising our delegated authority to interpret ambiguous terms in the Communications Act, as confirmed by the Supreme Court in *Brand X*, today's Order concludes that the facts in the market today are very different from the facts that supported the Commission's 2002 decision to treat cable broadband as an information service" (FCC, 2015, Feb. 26, p. 14).

Therefore, when opponents of the 2015 Open Internet Order argue that the FCC has no authority to reclassify broadband under Title II as a telecommunication service, they betray a shallow understanding of the *Brand X* decision. The FCC may have classified broadband one way for years, but that classification is theirs to make—or, as is now the case, to remake.

IV. Popular and Political Pressures for Net Neutrality.

Popular Pressure. The FCC's exercise of its authority to reclassify broadband, however, did not take place without pressures from inside and outside the agency. Aside from being a solution to recurring legal difficulties, it was a response to popular pressure. As FCC Chairman Tom Wheeler would state when the 2015 Order was announced,

"We heard from startups and world-leading tech companies. We heard from ISPs, large and small. We heard from public-interest groups and public-policy think tanks. We heard from Members of Congress, and, yes, the President. Most importantly, we heard from nearly 4 million Americans who overwhelmingly spoke up in favor of preserving a free and open Internet" (FCC, 2015, p.1).

This overwhelming support, however, was not unanimous. As *The Wall Street Journal* reported, "more than 100 Internet companies" including Amazon, Google, and Facebook united to send Wheeler a letter that his plans would threaten the Internet, not benefit it (Nagesh, 2014). Nevertheless, Internet communities such as Reddit would champion the cause, at one time "making over 15,000 calls in a span of just three hours" to the FCC and congressional representatives (Alexis, 2015). In April 2014, Josh Levy of Free Press joined with David Segal (Demand Progress), Amalia Deloney (Center for Media Justice), Sarah Morris (Open Technology Institute) and first-amendment lawyer Marvin Ammori to host a Reddit discussion forum, explain what was at stake with net neutrality, and urge users to get politically involved by contacting their representatives and the FCC directly (Levy, 2014). What was the result of these digital grass-roots campaigns? By September 2014, *The Washington Post* reported the FCC had received a record-breaking 3 million comments on net neutrality (Fung, 2014).

Presidential Pressure. If popular movements built pressure from the bottom, the executive branch applied pressure from the top. As the ACLU reported in *Network Neutrality 101*, the Bush-era FCC's classification of broadband as an information service, exempt from common carriage requirements, was challenged in the Supreme Court, but the Court deferred to the FCC and allowed the exemption (Stanley, 2010, p. 14). Events would take a different course following the end of the Bush presidency, though the FCC's vote on the 2015 Order split along party lines, with Republicans against it and Democrats for it.

In a shift from the previous presidential stance, President Barack Obama voiced support for the idea of a free and open internet, lending credence to the FCC's efforts. In November 2014, President Obama urged the FCC "to adopt the 'strongest possible rules' on net neutrality", specifically including the classification of "high-speed broadband service as a utility under Title II" (Ruiz, 2015). *The New York Times* quoted President Obama as saying, "For most Americans, the Internet has become an essential part of everyday communication and everyday life" (ibid). The idea that the Internet has become such an integral part of daily American life, to the same extent that other utilities like electricity and running water have, bolsters the idea that it should be regulated as such. It has become, for many, a necessity rather than a luxury good.

But President Obama's influence on the 2015 Order began much earlier. He furthered this reclassification agenda when he nominated businessman and former communications industry lobbyist Tom Wheeler to the FCC in May 2013 (White House, 2013). Less than a year later, Wheeler would assume the position of Chairman.

Internal Pressure. Tom Wheeler's becoming the FCC Chairman in November 2013, marks a major turning point in the net neutrality saga. Wheeler joined the FCC at a time when, within the agency, the idea of net neutrality had been gaining traction but failed to become fully realized. FCC efforts to promote net neutrality go back to 2005, when then-Chairman Kevin J. Martin spearheaded a policy statement about "Four Internet Freedoms" users were entitled to, including "access to any lawful content", and "benefit from competition among network providers" (Stanley, 2010, p. 16). This Internet Policy Statement was more an idea than an enforceable act. Although "the FCC maintained that it had sufficient authority to enforce the principles", the Statement "was not promulgated into regulation" (Ruane, 2014, p. 1). In fact, Comcast fought for its right to discriminate against certain forms of data in *Comcast vs. FCC*, and won the battle in the DC Circuit Court in 2010 (Stanley, 2010, p. 16).

The FCC tried again with The 2010 Open Internet Order. It attempted many of the same things the 2015 Order would set forth, but it faced a major problem. With broadband Internet access still classified as a Title I information service rather than a Title II telecommunication service, some aspects of the Order fell outside of the FCC's established authority. This explains the DC Circuit Court's 2014 decision, in *Verizon v. FCC*, to strike down the blocking and antidiscrimination provisions. The Court saw these provisions, though not the disclosure requirements, as imposing common carriage requirements on a non-telecommunication service (Jacobs, 2014, p. 1). In hindsight, it was the FCC's own classification scheme that made the 2010 Order lack teeth. Writing for the majority, Circuit Court Judge Tatel said,

"We think it obvious that the Commission would violate the Communications Act were it to regulate broadband providers as common carriers. Given the Commission's still-binding decision to classify broadband providers not as providers of 'telecommunciations services' but instead as providers of 'information services"... such treatment would run afoul of section 153(51): 'A telecommunications carrier shall be treated as a common carrier under this [Act] only to the extent that it is engaged in providing telecommunications services'" (Tatel, 2014, p. 45).

But alongside net neutrality, Chairman Wheeler also promoted the idea of broadband expansion on a national level, to bring high-speed Internet connections to underserved and rural areas. It makes sense to view these two priorities as two prongs of the same policy goal. Wheeler desires not only to make broadband a universal service for all citizens, but also to guarantee that service would provide unimpeded access to information on a nondiscriminatory, freely flowing basis.

Under the information service classification, broadband providers stood to create an even greater gap in the so-called digital divide between rich and poor, dividing internet access into "pay-to-play fast lanes for Internet and media companies that can afford it, and slow lanes for everyone else" (Ruiz, 2015). They could also act as censors, deciding what content their subscribers could access. This is no theoretical proposition, but one specifically argued for by plaintiffs in the 2015 case *United States Telecom Association v. FCC* who wish to block content they find objectionable. We shall look at this case in greater detail later.

Reclassifying broadband under Title II authority was the right policy move to achieve the FCC's goals. It would both eliminate the legal and litigation problems stemming from the vagueness of the 1996 Act, and clarify the FCC's authority to keep the ever-expanding broadband networks aligned with the populist goals of a free and open Internet. The complex prioritization schemes and companies' ability to effectively censor the Internet through throttling and blocking had no place in the future envisioned by

Chairman Wheeler and his supporters. The 2015 Open Internet Order aimed to secure the FCC's authority to guide the industry into this future.

V. Contentious Requirements of the 2015 Open Internet Order.

Clarifying Authority and Redefining Broadband. As we have seen, the FCC's vague Title I authority over information services has resulted in difficult legal battles and undermined its efforts to encourage broadband expansion. We need not reiterate the reclassification's significance here. But two points about this classification should be made before examining other aspects of the Order.

First, the FCC has decided to refrain or "forebear" from "enforcing provisions of Title II that are not relevant to modern broadband service", requirements normally faced by common carriage telecommunications service (FCC, 2015, Feb. 4). Many of these requirements developed in an age where the old copper-wire telephone network reigned supreme. Regulation evolved in the specific context of fostering competition in the telephone industry, seeking to restrain the monopolistic power of AT&T and its offspring the Bell companies, while simultaneously encouraging the entry of new companies into the market to spur innovation and keep prices low. Therefore, it would make little sense to suddenly subject all the existing broadband networks to provisions which were never intended to address their infrastructures, technologies, corporate structures, and competitive realities. (A complete table of these forebearances appears in *Highlights of the 2015 Open Internet Order*, pages 5-8. See Jacobs, Annotated Bibliography.)

Second, the Order treats broadband as having a download speed of 25Mbps or higher. This definition stems from the FCC's 2015 Broadband Progress Report (Singleton, 2015). Could this definition prove problematic? It seems, at first glance, the FCC has left a vast field of Internet service under the old classification, purely on the basis of speed. It makes little sense to define a connection speed of 24Mbps (or less) one way, and the same service (only faster) another way.

However, this problem is less about definition and more about focus. The FCC would like to see broadband access on a nationwide basis, and will push towards that future. In a 2014 hearing before the U.S. House Committee on Small Business, Chairman Wheeler made it clear that he did not consider 4Mbps fast enough at all, and he objected to subsidizing what he considered a sub-par speed (Brodkin, 2014). Therefore, Wheeler's FCC has chosen to focus on what may well become the new industry standard. As technology continues to increase bandwidth, we can anticipate the market will demand it. An internet connection of 25Mbps is already available from many cable providers, and even the wireless industry is looking to build more robust networks at that speed. AT&T recently announced a wireless broadband initiative intended to deliver speeds of 15Mbps to 25Mbps without relying on fixed-line cable infrastructure (Reed, 2015). Initiatives such as this may well serve Chairman Wheeler's intention of seeing broadband access for the entire nation. The FCC has chosen a forward-thinking definition of broadband so it may focus on these emerging technological advancements.

Service Requirements versus Free Speech Arguments. The 2015 Order deals with more than just the reclassification. It contains requirements aligned with the idea of net neutrality and the open exchange of information on the Internet. These include prohibitions against blocking any lawful content or unreasonably interfering with data transmission. These prohibitions seek to prevent Internet service providers from choosing what websites users may view on their network, and from throttling data from websites the ISP might not want to transmit. These prohibitions are bolstered with rules against impairing or degrading access to the Internet. These rules support a neutral net from the perspective of the information users can access unimpeded. The FCC also considered users by creating rules about mandatory disclosures aimed at making network management more transparent.

But these rules have met with an unexpected legal backlash. While advocates for "free speech" have long championed the net neutrality cause, members of the private, corporate sector have attempted to use free speech as an argument *against* the 2015 Order. In the words of Fred Campbell, executive director for the Center for Boundless Innovation in Technology, "A total ban on the editorial discretion of Internet service providers violates the First Amendment's command that Congress shall make no law abridging the freedom of the press" (Court Plans Speedy Review, 2015, p. 7). Campbell seems oblivious to the fact that the FCC is not Congress, and he confuses the FCC's prohibition against censorship with "leaving nothing to stop government censorship" of Internet speech (ibid).

But Campbell is not alone in making this duplicitous argument. Alamo Broadband, in a Joint Petition in a case involving the United States Telecom Association, asked the Court to review the FCC's 2015 Open Internet Order. The petitioners object to the Order on the grounds that 1) the Order's prohibition of blocking Internet content violates First Amendment "free speech" rights, 2) Section 706 of the Telecommunications Act does not authorize the kind of rules the Order creates, and 3) Sections 201(b) and 303(b) of the Act do not authorize the prohibition of paid prioritization agreements (Joint Brief, 2015, p. 12). The petitioners claim broadband providers "engage in speech" and exercise "editorial discretion" in deciding "which speech to transmit" (Joint Brief, 2015, p. 13). One might ask, "Which is it?" Is an ISP speaking, or is it transmitting speech?

The FCC responded that broadband providers are transmitters of other speakers, not speakers themselves, and this seems logically correct. The FCC's Brief in this case draws a clear distinction between subscribing to information sources such as *The Wall Street Journal*, which people recognize as a provider of *content*, and ordering broadband access from a cable company, which people understand as a "transmission service that supplies *access* to... content" (Brief, 2015, p. 24-25). The FCC's Brief points out that "Verizon's operation of *Huffington Post*, for example, is left untouched" because the FCC is not regulating content or speech (ibid, p. 25). Instead, the 2015 Order means subscribers to Verizon's *broadband* services will not have their access to other content blocked, regardless of whether or not Verizon owns such content providers or sanctions their views.

The petitioners further argue that their own First Amendment rights are violated because the FCC's anti-blocking rules "compel providers to carry all speech, including political speech with which providers disagree" (Joint Brief, 2015, p. 13). The petitioners wish to engage in blocking content with political views they find objectionable. In other words, the petitioners envision "free speech" as a state of affairs where they can block the speech of others, and object to the FCC's order to freely transmit all forms of lawful speech. The petitioners have turned the idea of "free speech" on its head by arguing that the First Amendment protects their ability to restrict the flow of ideas and dialogue in this nation. If this argument is typical of the private sector, then the FCC has done the right thing by stepping in now to prevent ISPs from becoming the *de facto* censors of the Internet.

Ending Paid Prioritization Agreements versus Broadband Expansion. Net neutrality encompasses more than neutrally handling data and website access. It also requires an end to the paid prioritization agreements which have long been promoted as necessary to maintaining service quality for real-time applications like streaming video. Ending paid prioritization carries with it economic and engineering concerns other aspects of the Order lack. Nearly everyone can understand that neutral handling of content removes from the networks the authority to censor content. Much of the popular support for net neutrality centers on anti-censorship and the American ideals of free speech and free expression. But prioritization touches on concerns which are less ideal and more practical.

By banning paid prioritization, the FCC has forced the issue of building more robust, high-speed broadband infrastructure. To avoid degradation in service quality, networks must incur greater expenses to build increased bandwidth. The Connect America Fund subsidizes these costs for networks willing to meet minimum speed requirements (Brodkin, 2014). To support experiments to bring broadband to rural areas, the FCC plans to release $100 million from the Fund, which is supported by the Universal Service program (Engebretson, 2014). Recent awards include more than $16 million to four companies in November 2015, with the goal of bringing broadband to areas in five states, and the FCC has planned a reverse auction for other carriers to step in (Arnason, 2015). The FCC clearly wants to stimulate broadband expansion, refusing to incentivize lower-capacity networks that could allow companies to profit from prioritization payments without increasing their capacity. After all, a scarcity of capacity forces the demand for prioritization, and generates a profit without improving infrastructure.

Wireless has a role to play in this broadband expansion. In the AT&T wireless broadband initiative mentioned earlier, we see an example of a possible solution to the expensive infrastructure problems posed by a prohibition on blocking and throttling. Bandwidth is not infinite, and if broadband companies seek to maintain quality of service in real-time streaming applications, they will need infrastructure that can meet those demands without restricting less time-sensitive data flows. Wireless broadband initiatives, if successful, may shift the economic pressure away from installing expensive last-mile fixed-line cable services. Instead, they will create a push for freeing up spectrum frequencies, which has been the goal of recent FCC spectrum auctions. The advantages to such auctions, though beyond the scope of this essay, are compelling enough that since the FCC began the first of more than thirty such auctions in 1994, the U.S. model has been emulated by many nations around the world pursuing the same spectrum usage goals (Cramton, 2001, p.1).

Reasonable Network Management Practices. With these arguments about prioritization versus expansion in mind, one other aspect of the 2015 Order bears examining. Because infrastructure expansion does not happen overnight, networks have received some wiggle room in the language of "reasonable" network management practices to ensure quality of service. The 2015 Order makes allowances for practices required to effectively manage a network, but what are these practices, and what is reasonable? As we have seen, leaving things to a judgment call often means that a federal judge will have to field these questions.

On the one hand, this sounds like the persistence of the same vague language which has plagued the FCC's efforts and undermined its authority for years. One can easily imagine a new glut of lawsuits asking state and federal judges to determine whether or not a management practice is reasonable—a seemingly endless exercise in subjectivity. But on the other hand, a one-size-fits-all definition of reasonable practices is a poor alternative. What may be reasonable with today's technology may cease to be reasonable as technology evolves, and it is a failure to allow for rapidly changing technology which has caused much of the legal problems under the 1996 Act.

Though Commissioner Maureen K. Ohlhausen of the Federal Trade Commission objects to the 2015 Order, she makes a good argument for the importance of deciding some matters on a case-by-case basis. Describing the "history of the FCC" as "a series of regulatory attempts... to fit new technologies and business models into an increasingly out-of-date regulatory model", she points out that "statutory, procedural, and resource constraints make it impossible for the FCC" to keep up with the "trends of a very complex and rapidly evolving industry" (Ohlhausen, 2015, p. 209). She then contrasts this with the FTC's "enforcement-centric rather than rule-making-centric" approach which allows it to address "deceptive or unfair practices" on a "case-by-case" basis instead of attempting to make one-size-fits-all rules (ibid, p. 212). Ohlhausen criticizes the 2015 Order's Title II reclassification of broadband for potentially reducing "the FTC's authority to protect consumers online" because common carrier services "are outside of the FTC's jurisdiction" (ibid, p. 229). But on the other hand, her admonitions to reduce the silos created by separate Titles and to adopt a more flexible, case-by-case approach suggest that the 2015 Order's requirement for undefined reasonability in network management is the right track for the FCC. If the FCC has decided it will be the agency to handle these matters, then it is doing the right thing by leaving itself room for flexibility instead of trying to rigidly define network management in an ever-changing world.

VI. Affirming the FCC's 2015 Open Internet Order.

A Clear and Current Standard of Authority. Given the difficult history of categorizing and regulating broadband Internet access, the FCC has made the right decision by bringing it under Title II authority. Technology has converged since the dawn of the Internet, but legal definitions and policies have failed to similarly converge. Federal regulation has lagged hopelessly behind technological advances which have reinvented and redefined the nature of telecommunications for the twenty-first century.

Regulating the various means of telecommunications based on the physical structures which originally carried them makes no sense in the digital age. All of the telecommunication services which originated on fixed-line, copper-wire, analog networks can now take place on digital networks, and so can all of the services formerly reliant on radio waves, as well as all services which began digitally. Regulation has treated differently the transmission of voice communication, audio entertainment, video conferencing, and Internet access as discretely different services based on a model of physical networks which no longer applies.

This increasingly nonsensical regulatory approach has plagued the courts long enough. It has wasted the time and resources of state and federal judges for decades, requiring them to interpret vague and poorly crafted laws. Judges have had to examine and re-examine the FCC's actions concerning highly technical matters more suited to engineers and economists, all in the context of outdated legislation which does not clearly apply to today's technology. The lack of legislative clarity about the FCC's proper scope of authority has resulted in expensive litigations that sap the energy of the FCC and the courts alike. The new Title II classification of broadband Internet access provides the agency a consistent and clear framework which, if not undermined by the courts and Congress, will greatly simplify the relevant legal questions and regulatory decisions.

Congress and the courts need to follow the FCC's lead in catching up with technological reality. This executive action gives a wake-up call to the legislative and judicial branches that times and technology have changed, and we cannot expect to efficiently regulate a new world using old and irrelevant approaches. Fortunately, judges at the state and federal level have expressed, even if only in dissenting opinions or in subsequently overruled decisions, a belief that broadband truly should be classified as a telecommunication service and not an information service. This bodes well for future judicial activity, as it shows many judges already favor this position, and have probably been wondering when the FCC would face facts.

Congress, on the other hand, subject to intense lobbying pressures from industry giants who have profited from the outdated classification regime, may be more reluctant to jump on the Title II bandwagon. It may be easier to get the nine justices of the Supreme Court to validate the 2015 Open Internet order than to build agreement amongst hundreds of legislators influenced by special interest groups.

Weathering the Legal Backlash. But even with the support of the other branches of government, the FCC's intended expansion of broadband Internet access will face obstacles. In Congress, the House Appropriations Committee recently confronted two amendments to the 2016 financial services and general government bill. As *Telecommunications Reports* explained, these amendments, which the Committee rejected, would have barred the FCC from implementing the 2015 Order until pending court cases had been resolved, prevented the FCC from using fiscal year 2016 funding "to directly or indirectly regulate charges or data usage limits for broadband Internet access" (including doing so through "enforcement actions"), and prohibited the FCC from enforcing any rule it had not published on its website "not later than 21 days before the date on which the vote occurs" (Kirby, 2015, p. 22). Clearly, congressional opponents of the 2015 Order were not above loading a general spending bill with ammunition against the FCC.

The FCC also had to deal with a number of requests to stay the Order, requests made by corporations in the Internet industry such as U.S. Telecom Association, AT&T, and CenturyLink; American Cable Association and the National Cable Association; and Daniel Berninger of the Voice Communications Exchange Committee (FCC Denies Requests, 2015, p. 15). The FCC denied them on the basis that "no irreparable harm" to the broadband companies had been shown. The parties to these denied requests then turned them into lawsuits for the Circuit Court to wade through. Ignoring the *Brand X* decision that the classification of broadband was the FCC's to decide, these companies argued that "broadband Internet access 'fits squarely' within the statutory definition of Communication Act Title I information services" (ibid). One of these cases is the US Telecom Association case covered in the previous section on "free speech" arguments.

On top of that, states have begun to challenge the FCC's decision, reached on the same day as the vote on the 2015 Order, to preempt state laws that have prevented municipalities from building their own broadband networks. On the forefront of this litigation stand Tennessee and North Carolina, each of which has limits on publicly created Internet service (Fung, 2015). In other areas, like the city of Chanute, Kansas, municipalities are taking it upon themselves to fill a service void left by broadband corporations (Lefler, 2014). While this approach fits in with Chairman Wheeler's vision of expanding broadband access, "nineteen states have such laws, often passed at the behest of private Internet service providers that didn't want to face competition" (Brodkin, 2015). The FCC may have achieved a more solid legal framework for its authority by reclassifying broadband, but its judicial battles are not yet over.

Leveling the Playing Field of Prioritization. The FCC has taken the right action to support worthy long-term goals, but the massive complexity of the infrastructure and political realities means neither a smooth nor unobstructed path in the short term.

In particular, doing away with paid prioritization challenges the status quo so deeply that it will produce both engineering and economic downsides. Despite these challenges, it is worth considering the flip side of the coin. Everyone wants their data transmitted at the best and fastest possible speed. No one wants to be left behind. Therefore, everyone has an interest in being prioritized. If we assume that everyone with such a desire can eventually muster the funds to pay for prioritization, then the logical result is the prioritization of everything.

In such a scenario, no one wins anything. The playing field would once again become level. Everyone paying for priority results in the same equality as no one paying for it; i.e., everyone gets the same treatment. Therefore, although paid prioritization makes sense at the outset when not everyone has paid for it yet, it wastes resources in a race that ultimately leads nowhere. The FCC's contentious ban on paid prioritization makes more sense in this light. The ban merely prevents this nonsensical and utterly doomed race to nowhere, and instead forces attention on how we can build more robust networks in an atmosphere of equal treatment and innovation.

VII. Conclusion.

Those who value the Internet for free and open access to data, information, and connection to others at reasonable prices will agree with the FCC's recent decision to bring broadband Internet under the umbrella of telecommunication services. By treating broadband access as a common carriage service, the FCC is in a greater position to prevent networks from censoring and limiting citizens' access to data—data we need to learn about and understand our increasingly complex world, and must increasingly rely on for our professional and economic well-being. Reclassifying broadband under Title II effectively solves a longstanding problem for the agency and federal courts.

Annotated Bibliography

Alexis [knothing]. (26 February, 2015). "Thank you, reddit. Your efforts led to an historic FCC ruling and this note from the President of the United States." *Blog.Reddit.* http://www.redditblog.com/2015/02/thank-you-reddit-your-efforts-led-to.html

   An example of online grass-roots political activism regarding net neutrality, and the high volume of response the FCC received as a result.

Arnason, Bernie. (16, November, 2015). "FCC Releases $16 Million for Rural Broadband Experiments Funding." *Telecompetitor.* http://www.telecompetitor.com/fcc-releases-16-million-for-rural-broadband-experiments-funding/

Brief for Respondents. (14 September, 2015). USCA Case #15-1063, *United States Telecom Association v. FCC.* Document #1573000. https://assets.documentcloud.org/documents/2423172/oifinal asfiled.pdf

   FCC responds to, among other things, the accusations of censorship and violations of First Amendment.

Brodkin, Jon. (17 September, 2014). "Sorry, AT&T and Verizon: 4Mbps isn't fast enough for 'broadband': FCC chairman says Americans shouldn't subsidize Internet service under 10Mbps." *ArsTechnica.* http://arstechnica.com/business/2014/09/sorry-att-and-verizon-4mbps-isnt-fast-enough-for-broadband/

   This article summarizes Chairman Wheeler's remarks before a House committee regarding a minimal acceptable speed for broadband Internet access, and its relation to subsidies from the Connect America Fund.

Brodkin, Jon. (26 February, 2015). "FCC overturns state laws that protect ISPs from local competition: Municipal broadband networks could expand because of FCC's controversial vote." *ArsTechnica.* http://arstechnica.com/business/2015/02/fcc-overturns-state-laws-that-protect-isps-from-local-competition/

Cramton, Peter. (February, 2001). Spectrum Auctions. In (2002) Cave, Martin, et. al., (Eds.), *Handbook of Telecommunications Economics, Vol. 1: Structure, Regulation, and Competition,* Chapter 14, pp. 605-639. Oxford, UK: Elsevier. http://www.cramton.umd.edu/papers2000-2004/01hte-spectrum-auctions.pdf

Cramton's chapter gives a history of spectrum auctions and their advantages to the public, corporations, and governments.

"Court Plans Speedy Review of Open Internet Order." (1 July, 2015). *Telecommunications Reports, 81*(13), 5-7.

Paragraphs 4-5: The DC Circuit Court in 2014 "overturned blocking and non-discrimination rules adopted in a 2010 FCC order as the impermissible application of de facto common carrier regulation to services that were not at the time classified as common carrier services" (p. 5). US Telecom Association and "other parties" requested the US Court of Appeals for the District of Columbia stay the 2015 reclassification of broadband as telecom, a stay which would therefore render the anti-blocking provisions unenforceable (p. 5).

The Court rejected this request but granted expedition in hearing *US Telecom Association v FCC* (case 15-1063) and similar cases to be consolidated. Page 7, paragraph 1 offers an argument that banning editorial discretion of ISPs equates to government censorship.

Engebretson, Joan. (12 November, 2014). "FCC: Rural Broadband Experiement Funding to Be Awarded in 'Coming Weeks'." *Telecompetitor*. http://www.telecompetitor.com/fcc-rural-broadband-experiment-funding-awarded-coming-weeks/

"FCC Denies Requests to Stay Open Internet Order for Not Citing 'Concrete' Harms; Eyes Turn to Court." (15 May, 2015). *Telecommunications Reports, 81*(10), 15-16.

Some stay requests mentioned in "Court Plans Speedy Review of Open Internet Order" were originally stay requests to the FCC by the companies who later filed with the DC Circuit: US Telecom Association, AT&T, and CenturyLink; American Cable Association and the National Cable Association; and Daniel Berninger of the Voice Communications Exchange Committee.

The article clarifies aspects of Title II regulation historically applied to telephone companies but which are not being applied to broadband access under the new Order, "including rate regulations, tariffing, last-mile unbundling, and obligations to contribute to the Universal Service Fund" (p. 15, column 1, last paragraph).

Joint petitioners in subsequent stay requests to the Circuit Court object, in part, to the reclassification "because broadband Internet access 'fits squarely' within the statutory definition of Communication Act Title I information services" (p. 15, column 2, third paragraph column 2). Article quotes the FCC's brief which denies "irreparable harm" to the broadband companies.

Federal Communications Commission. (4 February, 2015). *Chairman Wheeler Proposes New Rules for Protecting the Open Internet*. https://www.fcc.gov/document/chairman-wheeler-proposes-new-rules-protecting-open-internet

Statement of proposal to reclassify broadband access under Title II.

Federal Communications Commission. (adopted 26 February, 2015; released 12 March, 2015). *FCC-15-24A1: Report and Order on Remand, Declaration Ruling, and Order* (Commonly called the 2015 Open Internet Order).
https://apps.fcc.gov/edocs_public/attachmatch/FCC-15-24A1.pdf

Full text of the 2015 Open Internet Order.

Federal Communications Commission. (February, 2015). *Statement of Chairman Tom Wheeler RE: Protecting and Promoting the Open Internet, GN Docket No. 14-28.*
https://apps.fcc.gov/edocs_public/attachmatch/DOC-332260A2.pdf

Wheeler's statement briefly explains the new Title II classification of broadband, and summarizes the main "bright-line" rules of the 2015 Order.
See also the FCC's summary of the 2015 Order: (26 February, 2015). *FCC Adopts Strong, Sustainable Rules to Protect the Open Internet.*
https://www.fcc.gov/document/fcc-adopts-strong-sustainable-rules-protect-open-internet
See also the FCC Open Internet Webpage at
https://www.fcc.gov/openinternet
"Bright-line" rules summarized as:
• **No Blocking:** broadband providers may not block access to legal content, applications, services, or non-harmful devices.
• **No Throttling:** broadband providers may not impair or degrade lawful Internet traffic on the basis of content, applications, services, or non-harmful devices.

- **No Paid Prioritization:** broadband providers may not favor some lawful Internet traffic over other lawful traffic in exchange for consideration of any kind—in other words, no "fast lanes." This rule also bans ISPs from prioritizing content and services of their affiliates.

Fung, Brian. (15 September, 2014). "The FCC has now received 3 million net neutrality comments." *The Washington Post.* https://www.washingtonpost.com/news/the-switch/wp/2014/09/15/the-fcc-has-now-received-3-million-net-neutrality-comments/

Fung, Brian. (9 November, 2015). Obama championed cheap, fast, city-run Internet. His administration won't." *The Washington Post.* https://www.washingtonpost.com/news/the-switch/wp/2015/11/09/the-fccs-intervention-on-city-run-broadband-may-be-in-trouble/

Jacobs, Rebecca, and Palchick, Mark. (4 May, 2015). "Highlights of the 2015 Open Internet Order." *Wombe Carlye* (Client Report). http://www.wcsr.com/resources/pdfs/telecomm050414.pdf

Executive summary of the main points of the 2015 Order, including what the Order does not apply to (such as premises operators, dial-up, etc.). This report clarifies that broadband will be subject to sections 201, 202, and 208 of the Communications Act; privacy requirements of Section 222; and the disability provisions of 225, 251(a)(2), and 255. It explains that ISPs are required to comply with Section 254 (provides for promoting universal broadband) but not to contribute to the Universal Service Fund. Includes a table showing what Sections "forebearance" applies to.

Joint Brief for Petitioners Alamo Broadband Inc. and Daniel Berninger. (30 July, 2015). USCA Case #15-1063, *United States Telecom Association v. FCC.* Document #1565433.

https://assets.documentcloud.org/documents/2423210/alamo-net-neutrality-brief.pdf

Full text of the Joint Brief. The petitioners argue, among other things, that the FCC's new rules prohibiting them from effectively censoring by blocking content actually equate to censorship in violation of the First Amendment.

Kirby, Paul. (1 July, 2015). "House Appropriations Committee Retains Open Internet Order Stay." *Telecommunications Reports*, 81(13), 22-24.

Explains some Congressional response to the 2015 Order; namely, the addition (and subsequent rejection) of anti-FCC amendments to a spending bill.

Lefler, Dion. (24 May, 2014). "Chanute aims to provide speedy Internet service to all homes, businesses in town." *Wichita Eagle*. http://www.kansas.com/news/article1144149.html

Levy, Josh. (24 April, 2014). "We are fighting to restore Net Neutrality. Ask us anything. (Josh Levy from Free Press, David Segal from Demand Progress, Amalia Deloney of Center for Media Justice, First Amendment lawyer Marvin Ammori & Sarah Morris of Open Technology Institute)." *Reddit.* Archived post https://www.reddit.com/r/IAmA/comments/23vddm/we_are _fighting_to_restore_net_neutrality_ask_us

Nagesh, Gautham. (7 May, 2014). Amazon, Google, Facebook and Others Disagree With FCC Rules on Net Neutrality: Firms, Commissioners Voice Concerns With New Rules That Threaten 'Net Neutrality'." *The Wall Street Journal.* http://www.wsj.com/news/articles/SB1000142405270230370130 4579548364154205126

Nuechterlein, Jonathan E., and Weiser, Philip J. (2013). *Digital Crossroads: Telecommunications Law and Policy in the Internet Age. 2ⁿᵈ Edition*. Cambridge, MA: MIT Press.

College textbook with an excellent background on the technology of the Internet, along with the political and legal environment of regulating it. Although it examines the history of the net neutrality movement, the book admits that at the time of publication, much remained to be settled in the courts and at the FCC. The issuance of the 2015 Order settled many of the questions posed in the text.

Ohlhausen, Maureen K. (April, 2015). "The FCC's Knowledge Problem: How to Protect Consumers Online." *Federal Communications Law Journal*, 67(2), 204-234. http://www.fclj.org/wp-content/uploads/2015/09/67.2.2_Ohlhausen.pdf

In 2006, author was Director of the Federal Trade Commission's Office of Policy Planning, leading the FTC's inquiry into net neutrality, which produced the 2007 report "Broadband Connectivity Competition Policy". Pages 208-212 summarize the problems of trying to regulate the modern telecom/internet environment, which is perpetually changing, with one-size-fits-all rules that cannot help but lag behind industry realities.

Chapter 2 addresses net neutrality and the FCC. 2A sums up the major arguments for and against net neutrality. 2B reviews the history of classifying always-on cable Internet access as an information service under Title I; the Verizon decision striking down the anti-blocking aspects of the 2010 Open Internet Order; and the development of the 2015 Order. Chapter 3A critiques specific provisions of the 2015 Order, pointing out that paid prioritization has benefits.

Author argues that reclassifying broadband under Title II (common carrier) removes it from FTC jurisdiction, although the FTC leads the world in privacy and data security enforcement, and has protected consumers many times from deceptive or unfair behaviors of broadband providers.

Reed, Brad. (1 October, 2015). "AT&T Is Testing New Tech That Delivers Home Broadband Service Wirelessly." *BGR (Boy Genius Report)*. http://bgr.com/2015/10/01/att-fixed-wireless-broadband-test/

Ruane, Kathleen Ann. (26 March, 2014). *Net Neutrality: The FCC's Authority to Regulate Broadband Internet Traffic Management.* (CRS Report R40234). Congressional Research Service. https://www.fas.org/sgp/crs/misc/R40234.pdf

Author is a legislative attorney. The report was prepared for members and committees of Congress and published a year before the 2015 Order. It examines the 2010 Order and the subsequent *Verizon v FCC* case. The DC Circuit Court in *Verizon* found that the 2010 Order's anti-discrimination and anti-blocking provisions exceeded the FCC's Title I authority over "information services", which was the FCC's current classification of broadband. See page 4, paragraph 1 for an analysis of *Brand X* where the Supreme Court decided the FCC could classify broadband.

The report gives a succinct history of the classification of broadband and its relation to the Telecommunications Act (Section 706, specifically), Title I ("ancillary" authority), and Title II (common carrier). See pages 9-10 for a highlight of relevant passages from Section 706. See page 12 for a summary of what "common carrier" means.

Ruiz, Rebecca R., and Lohr, Steve. (26 Feb., 2015). "FCC Approves Net Neutrality Rules, Classifying Broadband Internet Service as a Utility". *The New York Times.* http://www.nytimes.com/2015/02/27/technology/net-neutrality-fcc-vote-internet-utility.html?_r=0

Signaigo, Amy L. (Spring, 2007). National Cable & Telecommunications Association v. Brand X Internet Services: Resolving Irregularities in Regulation? *Northwestern Journal of Technology and Intellectual Property*, 5(2): Article 8 (PDF not paginated). http://scholarlycommons.law.northwestern.edu/cgi/viewcont ent.cgi?article=1147&context=njtip

> Author was a JD candidate at Northwestern University School of Law, with a background in hardware engineering and a Bachelor's in Computer and Electrical Engineering from Purdue. The article examines *Brand X*. It explains why the Ninth Circuit Court applied the *Portland* decision rather than *Chevron*; *Portland* being its own ruling that broadband was a telecom service not an information service.
>
> Section IV examines the difficulties of this case, especially how they stem from the classifications of telecommunications versus information services, and it argues the classifications need changed or eliminated. Section V offers a critique of inconsistencies within FCC broadband policy.

Singleton, Micah. (29 January, 2015). "The FCC has changed the definition of broadband: The minimum broadband download speeds now begin at 25Mbps, up from 4Mbps." *The Verge.* http://www.theverge.com/2015/1/29/7932653/fcc-changed-definition-broadband-25mbps

Stanley, Jay. (October, 2010). Network Neutrality 101: *Why the Government Must Act to Preserve the Free and Open Internet.* American Civil Liberties Union (ACLU). https://www.aclu.org/files/assets/ACLU_report_-_Network_Neutrality_101_October_2010.pdf

Tatel, David S. (14 January, 2014). United States Court of Appeals for the District of Columbia Circuit. *Verizon v. Federal Communications Commission*, 740 F.3d 623, 11-1355.

https://www.cadc.uscourts.gov/internet/opinions.nsf/3af8b4d
938cdeea685257c6000532062/$file/11-1355-1474943.pdf

Thomas, Clarence. (27 June, 2005). United States Supreme Court.
*National Cable & Telecommunications Ass'n v. Brand X
Internet Services*, 545 U.S. 967. (Justice Thomas for the
majority, Justice Scalia dissenting.)
http://www.techlawjournal.com/courts2003/brandx/brandx_s
cus.pdf

United States Congress. (3 January, 1996). *Telecommunications
Act of 1996*. http://transition.fcc.gov/Reports/tcom1996.pdf

White House, Office of the Press Secretary. (9 May, 2013).
"Presidential Nominations Sent to the Senate."
WhiteHouse.Gov. https://www.whitehouse.gov/the-press-
office/2013/05/09/presidential-nominations-sent-senate-0

4

Case Study:
Brand X

I. Background and Summary of Case.

In February 2015, the FCC released the 2015 Open Internet Order. Among other things, the Order reclassified broadband Internet access as a telecommunications service subject to common carrier regulation under the FCC's Title II authority, pursuant to authority granted by the Telecommunications Act of 1996. Litigation in federal courts has already begun to challenge the FCC's new regulatory scheme, including the FCC's authority to change broadband's existing classification from an information service regulated under Title I (in which it was not subject to common carrier regulatory practices).

However, *Brand X* clarifies the Supreme Court's perception of this authority. Although in *Brand X* the Court upheld the FCC's authority to classify broadband as an information service and not a telecommunications service, the rationale of the majority opinion clearly supports the opposite decision, too. *Brand X* recognizes the FCC's authority to make this decision, regardless of which way it decides to classify.

The opinion discussed in this case study was issued concurrently on June 17, 2005 with the certiorari on *Federal Communications Commission et al v. Brand X Internet Services et al.* It reverses the decision of the Ninth Circuit Court of Appeals which had ruled against the FCC's classification of broadband as an information service. The Ninth Circuit had reasoned that because cable modems used telecommunications technology, classifying broadband as telecommunication service was the *best* interpretation of The Telecommunications Act of 1996. The Ninth Circuit reasoned that since the FCC did not make the best interpretation, the agency's classification could be struck down by the court. Supreme Court Justice Thomas' majority opinion found fault with the Ninth Circuit's reasoning.

II. Major Points of Reasoning.

The majority found the FCC's construction of language from the Telecommunications Act of 1996 to be well within its lawful authority. Much of the opinion provides a primer on internet technology, both emerging and converging at that time. It gives the appropriate technological and policy background for why the thorny distinctions between "information" and "telecommunication" services exist in the first place. Given the complexity of this discussion, it suffices to say it allowed the Court to assert that the FCC's interpretation of The Act was, in fact, reasonable. That it may not have been the *best* or even the *only* interpretation was beside the point to the Court, so long as it was *reasonable*.

In terms of precedent, the Court disapproved of the Ninth Circuit's use of *AT&T Corp. v. Portland* which held that cable modem was a telecommunications service. The Court asserted that the proper precedent to use was *Chevron*. The Court's reasoning began first with establishing the ambiguity of The Act, an ambiguity immediately obvious upon *any* reading of the legislation, and a persistent regulatory problem in more cases than this one.

The Court then uses this ambiguity to establish *Chevron* as the correct precedent in such a case: "If a statute is ambiguous, and if the implementing agency's construction is reasonable, *Chevron* requires a federal court to accept the agency's construction of the statute, even if the agency's reading differs from what the court believes is the best statutory interpretation. *Id.*, at 843-844, and n. 11" (Thomas, 2005, p. 8).

Therefore, the majority opinion in *Brand X* clearly established:
1. The Telecommunications Act of 1996 is ambiguous regarding the definitions and classifications of "telecommunications services" versus "information services", and

2. This ambiguity affords the FCC the authority to classify the services and create regulation based on a reasonable interpretation of the given wording, and

3. This interpretation does *not* need to agree with any particular court's preferred reading of the ambiguity but must only be reasonable, and

4. In such a scenario where a court might read The Act differently than the FCC might, the courts must defer to the FCC (per *Chevron*).

In short, the FCC has authority under the ambiguous terms of the Telecommunications Act of 1996 to classify cable modem internet access as either information service (regulated under Title I) *or* telecommunications service (regulated under Title II) as it sees fit. Therefore, when considering the 2015 Open Internet Order, it is entirely reasonable to accept the FCC's authority to now reclassify broadband as a telecommunications service (Title II) despite its earlier classification to the contrary, for this classification power rightly belongs to the FCC.

III. Dissenting Opinion.

Justice Scalia's dissenting opinion focuses on his belief that because a cable modem has a telecommunications function, it by definition renders broadband cable Internet access a telecommunications service. This contrasts with majority arguments that the essential service provided as broadband Internet access is, by definition, an information service, and the modem is simply a functionally inseparable tool for providing the actual underlying service.

Scalia's dissent also argued that the "*Chevron* deference" to agency interpretation gave federal agencies a dangerous amount of power to take "action that the Supreme Court found unlawful" by creating an environment where "judicial decisions" are "subject to reversal by Executive officers" (p. 14, p. 13).

IV. Conclusion.

If the distinction between "information" and "telecommunication" services appears confusing and arbitrary, it is exactly this artificial and legally cumbersome distinction between converging technologies the 2015 Open Internet Order seeks to eliminate. While the majority may have been correct on their legal definitions, Scalia too was correct in his insight that these technologies could not logically or meaningfully be separated.

The FCC's interpretation of its authority pursuant to *Brand X* agrees with this analysis. Section C.43 of the 2015 Order refers to both the majority and dissenting opinions of this case.

References

Federal Communications Commission. (adopted 26 February, 2015; released 12 March, 2015). *FCC-15-24A1: Report and Order on Remand, Declaration Ruling, and Order* (Commonly called the 2015 Open Internet Order). https://apps.fcc.gov/edocs_public/attachmatch/FCC-15-24A1.pdf

Panner, Owen M. (3 June, 1999). *AT&T Corp. v. City of Portland*, 43 F. Supp. 2d 1146 (D. Or. 1999). https://www.courtlistener.com/opinion/2423001/at-t-corp-v-city-of-portland/

Stevens, John Paul. (25 June, 1984). United States Supreme Court. *Chevron USA Inc. v Natural Resources Defense Council, Inc.*, 467 U.S. 837. https://www.law.cornell.edu/supremecourt/text/467/837

Thomas, Clarence. (27 June, 2005). United States Supreme Court. *National Cable & Telecommunications Ass'n v. Brand X Internet Services*, 545 U.S. 967. (Justice Thomas writing for the majority, Justice Scalia dissenting.) http://www.techlawjournal.com/courts2003/brandx/brandx_scus.pdf

5

The FCC's Spectrum Auctions:
Challenges and Advantages

I. Introduction.

The use of the electromagnetic spectrum to transmit data has evolved significantly. Wireless transmission has extensively replaced wire-based telephones in telecommunications, especially for individual use. On the other hand, television broadcasting has largely adopted cable wires, transitioning away from using the spectrum for wireless transmission. Federal policymakers, viewing spectrum as a finite resource, have allocated certain frequencies of the spectrum to different uses. As technology changes, the federal government auctions frequencies to make them available for new uses. This method presents some challenges, but it also holds some advantages over the earlier methods by which spectrum was re-allocated.

II. Differences in the 2008 and 2015 Auctions.

2015's AWS-3 auction covered 65 MHz of spectrum, divided amongst 1,614 licenses (Goldstein, 2014). This auction dealt with different blocks of the spectrum than the 2008 auction. 2008's auction involved the 700 MHz portion of the spectrum. The upper and lower portions of the 700 MHz band "had previously been occupied by UHF television channels between 52 and 69" (Nuechterlein, 2013, p. 134). This year's AWS auction addresses blocks in the 1695-1710, 1755-1780, and 2155-2180 MHz bands. The 1755-1780 MHz band is used by a number of government agencies for purposes including activity related to national security, and weaning the government off these frequencies to free them up for private use is a process fraught with enormous technological problems and costs (ibid, p. 134).

III. Transitional Challenges.

Because the spectrum being auctioned is still in use by government agencies that are not prepared to give them up yet, the bidders have won things they cannot yet use. "The thorniest part of the auction process will likely be relocating government users from the spectrum or having carriers share the spectrum with government users," and this will be managed by a transition plan from the National Telecommunications & Information Administration, part of the U.S. Department of Commerce (Goldstein, 2014). To resolve this disadvantage takes more than a plan. It takes funding. This explains the reserve prices at spectrum auctions. The reserve prices were set high enough to make sure "the FCC raised enough money to cover relocation costs for government users of the spectrum" (ibid).

IV. Anti-Competitive Challenges.

One regulatory disadvantage becomes clear when looking at the big players in these auctions. The FCC is selling these spectrum bands to the very same companies whose expansions and mergers they have been monitoring and, in many cases, denying. Take Verizon as an example. In 2006, Verizon Wireless announced it would "purchase all the spectrum that various cable companies had acquired in the 2006 AWS auction but had never put to use" (Nuechterlein, 2013, p. 158). The FCC conditionally approved this deal, despite controversy, so this portion of the spectrum would not go unused (ibid). Verizon subsequently became the "only wireless operator to win a nationwide license in the 700MHz auction in 2008" (Reardon, 2015). And it continues to add spectrum now, having bid more than $10 billion in this year's AWS-3 auction (Seifert, 2015). These bids earned Verizon 181 licenses, increasing its AWS coverage of the US from 70 percent of the U.S. population to around 95 percent, with a "combination of at least 40 MHz of AWS-1 or AWS-3 spectrum in 92 of the top 100 U.S. markets" (Goldstein, 2015). Though the increased coverage may bode well for Verizon subscribers, it is difficult to reconcile this expansion with the earlier controversy. The FCC may have reason to worry about its auctions' effects if they expand the same companies it monitors for monopolistic practices.

The big winner of this year's AWS auction, AT&T, illustrates the problem further. Bidding "nearly $18.2 billion for 251 licenses", AT&T gained more licenses than the closest three competitors: Dish, Verizon, and T-Mobile (Seifert, 2015). While the FCC approved AT&T's merger with Cingular in 2004, the FCC rejected AT&T's merger with T-Mobile in 2011. Again, it is difficult to reconcile the FCC's willingness to sell off large portions of the spectrum to the same companies it is trying to keep from getting so big they become anti-competitive. The philosophy that guides this balancing act seems to be that the FCC "will go to great lengths to free up more capacity for use by mobile wireless providers, but probably not at the expense of losing a major national carrier" (Nuechterlein, 2013, p.158).

V. Economic Challenges.

Auctions also present a problem for economies if speculative bidding drives up the cost of licenses to an unreasonable amount. For example, a European auction in 2000 pushed up bids on broadband spectrum so high that it "eventually bankrupted some of the auction winners and sent the European wireless industry into a tailspin" (ibid, p. 95). However, poor auction design was partly to blame, not just speculative zeal (ibid.). Clearly, a well-designed auction can combat this disadvantage.

But, as the FCC learned with NextWave Communications in the 1990s, a bid does not guarantee the ability to pay. NextWave, in the throes of bankruptcy, defaulted on its installment payments for licenses it had won in auction. The spectrum blocks it had won remained unused as the gears of litigation slowly ground, achieving the opposite of the goal of freeing up the spectrum (ibid, p. 95-6). To combat this disadvantage, bidders must be qualified prior to auctions (FCC Auctions Home). This year's AWS auction had more than 70 qualified bidders

(Goldstein, 2014). The FCC establishes and publishes this list of qualified bidders, including the range of credit extended to them (FCC, 2014, p. 1-4). Clearly the FCC wants to vet the credit of its bidders and avoid the disadvantages caused with NextWave.

VI. Advantages.

Despite these administrative and regulatory challenges, the auction method presents some clear advantages over earlier methods of spectrum re-allocation. These advantages are so compelling that since the FCC began the first of more than thirty such auctions in 1994, the U.S. model has been emulated by many nations around the world pursuing the same spectrum usage goals (Cramton, 2001, p.1). Previously, the FCC had used either comparative hearings or lotteries (ibid, p. 2). Countries that have not followed the FCC's continually-improving auction model "have suffered from inefficient license assignments and other flaws" (ibid). For bidders, the advantages include the ability to "build packages of complementary licenses using the information revealed" in the bidding process, and the opportunity to shift their bids in the process to a license that might "represent a better value" (ibid.).

The FCC enjoys the advantage of doing away with the comparative hearing process which was "expensive, standardless, and time-consuming," a "beauty contest" rife with favoritism for the big incumbents and "those with political ties" (Nuechterlein, 2015, p. 92-3). The FCC also avoids the numerous disadvantages of the lottery system it experimented with beginning in 1984. Lotteries were not only random but generated so many hundreds of thousands of applicants that the paperwork partially collapsed the facility which housed them (ibid, p. 93). The lotteries also suffered from a design which allowed the winners to resell their spectrum rights, often for enormous sums which benefitted those companies but ultimately deprived the U.S. Treasury of revenue it could have gained at an auction (ibid, p. 93-4).

VII. Conclusion.

Due to the overwhelming advantages spectrum auctions have for all parties, including bidders, regulators, consumers, administrators, and the economy, they are the best method available for re-allocating spectrum for new and different uses. The academic community and the international community agree, and many nations have benefitted from adopting similar models. The disadvantages of the auction method are several, but the FCC has been improving the auction process in response to the occasional failures of the system both domestically and abroad.

References

Cramton, Peter. (February, 2001). Spectrum Auctions. In (2002) Cave, Martin, et. al., (Eds.), *Handbook of Telecommunications Economics, Vol. 1: Structure, Regulation, and Competition*, Chapter 14, pp. 605-639. Oxford, UK: Elsevier. http://www.cramton.umd.edu/papers2000-2004/01hte-spectrum-auctions.pdf

Federal Communications Commission. *FCC Auctions Home*. http://wireless.fcc.gov/auctions/default.htm?job=auctions_home

Federal Communications Commission. (30 October, 2014). *FCC AWS-3 Auction, Auction ID: 97, Qualified Bidders (Attachment A)*. http://transition.fcc.gov/Daily_Releases/Daily_Business/2014/db1030/DA-14-1564A2.pdf

Goldstein, Phil. (12 November, 2014). "AWS-3 spectrum aution primer: What you need to know before the bidding starts." *FierceWireless*. http://www.fiercewireless.com/special-reports/aws-3-spectrum-auction-primer-what-you-need-know-bidding-starts

Goldstein, Phil. (17 February, 2015). "Verizon: With AWS-3, we have at least 40 MHz of AWS spectrum in 92 of top 100 markets." *FierceWireless*. http://www.fiercewireless.com/story/verizon-aws-3-we-have-least-40-mhz-aws-spectrum-92-top-100-markets/2015-02-17

Nuechterlein, Jonathan E., and Weiser, Philip J. (2013). *Digital Crossroads: Telecommunications Law and Policy in the Internet Age. 2nd Edition*. Cambridge, MA: MIT Press.

Reardon, Marguerite. (29 January, 2015). "FCC rakes in $45 billion from wireless spectrum auction: The record-breaking auction highlights the demand for high-speed wireless service and signals strong promise for the upcoming auction of TV broadcast spectrum." *CNet*. http://www.cnet.com/news/fcc-rakes-in-45-billion-from-wireless-spectrum-auction/

Seifert, Dan. (30 January, 2015). "AT&T emerges as big winner in FCC spectrum auction: Dish, Verizon also spent billions." *The Verge*. http://www.theverge.com/2015/1/30/7952941/at-t-largest-bidder-fcc-aws-3-wireless-spectrum-auction

6

Case Study:
Obergefell v. *Hodges*

I. Summary of Case and Decision.

This case addresses several cases consolidated by the Sixth Circuit Court where same-sex couples filed District Court suits when their States had either denied them marriage licenses or refused to recognize same-sex marriages performed lawfully in other States. The District Courts all ruled in favor of these people, but the Circuit Court reversed and ruled against them.

Associate Justice Kennedy's majority opinion reversed the Sixth Circuit Court's decision. The Supreme Court determined States must grant marriage licenses to same-sex partners and recognize the legality of same-sex marriages performed in other States, per the Fourteenth Amendment.

II. Opinion as to Jurisdiction and Justiciability.

The opinion asserts marriage is a fundamental civil right and therefore covered by the Fourteenth Amendment "guarantee of equal protection" as a fundamental constitutional right. The opinion argues the Court can strike down laws which create inequality even when such laws have not been previously challenged. The opinion rejects arguments that more debate and studies need to be done, arguing that a body of law and literature has sufficiently addressed the question, and that "individuals who are harmed need not await legislative action before asserting a fundamental right."

The Court refused to leave the fundamental right to marry in the hands of State legislatures because citizens were being denied Constitutionally-protected liberties. The opinion asserts this fundamentally constitutional matter falls within the jurisdiction of the Court and is entirely justiciable, not a matter which must await State legislation.

III. Opinion as to the Definition of Marriage.

The opinion's discussion of the definition of marriage is broken down into several arguments. First, the opinion rejects arguments that same-sex marriages demean marriage, reasoning that same-sex applicants clearly place a high value on marriage or else would not pursue it. Second, the opinion recognizes that the institution of marriage has greatly changed and been redefined throughout history, and the inclusion of same-sex partners is merely one more phase in that historical trend. (The opinion refers especially to prior laws banning inter-racial marriages, though it touches on other historical trends such as arranged marriage.) Finally, the opinion gives no credence to arguments on the immorality of homosexual acts, arguing instead that laws to that effect demean citizens.

IV. Opinion as to Marriage as a Constitutional Right.

Four principles support the opinion's assertion that marriage is a fundamental, constitutional right. First, the choice to marry is "inherent in the concept of individual autonomy." Second, marriage "supports a two-person union unlike any other in its importance to committed individuals." Third, marriage "safeguards children and families" by providing stability and dignity. (The court rejects arguments that intent to procreate is a qualification for marriage, reasoning that even opposite-sex unions may choose not to procreate.) Fourth, "marriage is a keystone of the Nation's social order" due to the role it plays legally and socially.

V. Dissenting Opinions.

Dissenting opinions claim the Court had the "power to say what the law is, not what it should be," denying arguments on the constitutionality of marriage rights. Dissenters argued marriage has "always been understood" as between a man and a woman, and was understood as such when the Fourteenth Amendment was ratified. Dissenters argued this core definition is not subject to change until State legislatures or public referenda redefine it through the democratic process. Dissenters argued the Court was not interpreting law but making policy, a job reserved for the legislature.

Dissenters found no merit in applying the Fourteenth Amendment to marriage, arguing that the judicial role is not to determine which rights are fundamental constitutional rights. Alito argued the constitution gives the people the right to determine what marriage is, not a fundamental right to marry regardless of gender. Thomas' dissent focuses on the definition of liberty in terms of the Due Process and Equal Protection clauses of the Fourteenth Amendment, and argues that denying same-sex marriages in no way infringes upon a citizen's liberty. He asserts that protected liberties are freedom *from* government interference, not necessarily freedom *to* do anything.

Dissenters argued that judicial precedent does not support the majority opinion, and the opinion is based solely on the majority's belief that same-sex couples should be able to marry.

VI. Conclusion.

Though I am glad for the Supreme Court's decision, the Dissenters have valid reservations about the Court's pushing the boundaries of its power. However, future generations will look back on this decision as favorably as *Brown v. Board of Education*, where the Court exercised power to strike down segregated education, or even Abraham Lincoln's decision to end the institution of slavery. Neither of these actions was viewed without dissent at the time. Yet progressive-minded people view them favorably, for they acted against discrimination, inequality, and bigotry.

A fully democratic process does little to prevent abuses of minorities. The majority can always vote to marginalize a minority group, and this is the weakness of leaving this matter to State legislatures. As long as the Supreme Court uses its power to provide equal civil rights, then I applaud its application of power. The letter of the law as to the boundaries of power will always be a subordinate concern to the primary questions of improving justice in a society based on equality and fairness.

References

Kennedy, Anthony M. (26 June, 2015). *Obergefell* v. *Hodges, Director, Ohio Department of Health, et al.,* 576 U.S. (2015). (Justice Kennedy for the majority; Justices Alito, Roberts, Scalia, and Thomas dissenting). http://www.supremecourt.gov/opinions/14pdf/14-556_3204.pdf

Appendix: Fourteenth Amendment

United States Constitution:
Amendment 14, Section 1 (of 5)

All persons born or naturalized in the United States, and subject to the jurisdiction thereof, are citizens of the United States and of the State wherein they reside. No State shall make or enforce any law which shall abridge the privileges or immunities of citizens of the United States; nor shall any State deprive any person of life, liberty, or property, without due process of law; nor deny to any person within its jurisdiction the equal protection of the laws.

Passed by Congress 13 June, 1866. Ratified 9 July, 1868.

7

Human Genes in the Global Market:
How Two Nations Reached Opposing Conclusions to the Myriad Genetics Case

Abstract

I. The Origins of Biological and Genetic Patents in the U.S.
II. The Origins of the Myriad Genetics Case in the U.S. and Abroad.
III. The Myriad Genetics Case in the U.S.
IV. The Origins of the Myriad Genetics Case in Australia.
V. The Decisions in the Myriad Case in Australia.
VI. Conclusion.

References

Abstract

The Myriad Genetics cases in the United States and Australia focus on patent control of two human gene sequences and the clinical methods of detecting them. Myriad Genetics patents refer to the genes as "17q-linked breast and ovarian cancer susceptibility gene" due to their location on the long arm of human chromosome 17. They received the names BRCA1 and BRCA2 from Mary Claire King, whose group at the University of California, Berkeley identified them in published research in 1990. Myriad Genetics' subsequent patent claims on BRCA1 and BRCA2 entered litigation in the US in 2009 and Australia in 2010, and met with dispute in the European Union and Canada. The US Supreme Court issued a final decision on the validity of the patent claims in 2013, reversing an earlier decision at the Circuit Court level which had, in turn, reversed an initial decision at the District Court level. The Federal Court of Australia's appeals court reached a judgment in September 2014 upholding a Federal Court decision from 2013. While the US Supreme Court invalidated the patents covering the gene sequence, the Australian courts upheld them. The differences in both the legal precedents and the patent terminology in each country have a direct bearing on why such opposing decisions happened. The political and economic realities of today's globalized business environment also influenced the decisions. To the extent that patents help enforce intellectual property rights, understanding how each nation came to its decision provides insight into the role of human genetic material in today's global information society.

Keywords: BRCA1, BRCA2, discovery, genes, European Patent Office, Federal Court of Australia, Genetic Technologies, intellectual property, invention, litigation, Myriad Genetics, patent, US Supreme Court.

I. The Origins of Biological and Genetic Patents in the U.S.

The 2013 decision by the U.S. Supreme Court in *Association for Molecular Pathology v. Myriad Genetics, Inc.* definitively concluded four years of mixed judicial response to the case. Myriad's patents became invalid at the District Court level in 2010, but the Court of Appeals for the Federal Circuit reversed this decision, returning Myriad's patent rights to them (Supreme Court Orders, 2012, p. 26). The Supreme Court, after ordering the Court of Appeals to review and reconsider its decision in 2012, eventually reversed the decision again, striking down the patents in 2013 just three years before they would have expired (Victory for Genes, 2013, p. 792). This mixed judicial response follows a pattern of conflicting U.S. court decisions about biological material, a pattern showing distinctly different agendas between the Supreme Court and the Circuit Court.

The legality of patenting natural genetic material first came into question in 1948 in a case concerning a combination of different bacteria which, when applied to seeds, assisted in nitrogen uptake in adult plants (Leal, 2014, p. 406). The Supreme Court ruled in *Funk Brothers Seed Co. v. Kalo Inoculant Co.* that, because all of the bacteria occurred naturally, they could not be patented (ibid, p. 407). The court's decision asserted the qualities of these naturally occurring bacteria "like the heat of the sun, electricity, or the qualities of metals, are part of the storehouse of knowledge of all men... manifestations of laws of nature, free to all men, and reserved exclusively to none" (Rogers, 2013, p. 446). Patents were intended to provide protection to inventions and inventors, and the court did not consider naturally occurring biological material to be an invention.

This decision showed consistency with an earlier case regarding biological material in 1874: *American Wood Paper Co. v. Fibre Disintegrating Co.* In that case, the Supreme Court "rejected a patent for cellulose isolated from nature" on the basis that extracting a natural substance by "decomposition or disintegration of material substances" did not render that biological substance eligible for patent (ibid, p. 444). This thinking foreshadowed the Supreme Court's 2013 decision in *Myriad*, summarized by Justice Clarence Thomas: "Myriad did not create or alter any of the genetic material in the BRCA1 and BRCA2 genes. The location and order of the nucleotides existed in nature before Myriad found them. Nor did Myriad create or alter the genetic structure of DNA" (Victory for Genes, 2013, p. 792).

Ten years later, however, in the 1958 case *Merck & Co. v. Olin Mathieson Chemical Corp.*, the court ruled in favor of patenting biological material concentrated or purified from its natural state (Leal, 2014, p. 407). This decision differed from *Funk Bros.* owing to the modification of the material, in this case vitamins and adrenalin, which brought the naturally occurring material into a new form. Subtle though the difference may be, the court's decision shows consistency with their earlier thinking: discovering a natural biological material does not make the material patent eligible, but inventing new forms of it could. The crux of the matter lies in the invention, not the discovery.

Two events in the 1980s reinforced this thinking but began a new stage in the patenting of biological material and organisms. The 1980 case *Diamond v. Chakrabaty* involved the creation of a new form of bacteria, one that did not occur naturally (ibid, p. 408). Here, the Supreme Court upheld its thinking on discovery versus invention. While the Funk Bros. case involved bacteria found in nature, the newly created bacteria in *Chakrabaty* qualified as an invention. The court ruled that "anything... made by man" could be eligible for patenting (ibid, p. 408). The Supreme Court split five-to-four on the *Chakrabaty* decision, but the deciding factor was the ability of the bacteria to decompose crude oil—ability not found in naturally occurring bacteria and thus qualifying for invention (Rogers, 2013, p. 448).

In 1987, this thinking found reinforcement in *Ex parte Allen*, a challenge to a rejection of a patent involving the genetic material of oysters wherein cell nuclei could be induced to contain "multiple DNA chromosomes of the same type" (Leal, 2014, p. 408). The Board of Patent Appeals and Interference referred to

Chakrabaty as precedent that, as an invention, genes and even whole organisms were patent-eligible. The United States Patent and Trademark Office (USPTO) issued a statement agreeing with this.

The Court of Appeals for the Federal Circuit which decided in Myriad's favor made a similar decision in 1993. In their ruling on *In re Bell*, the court disregarded the fact that DNA sequences occur naturally and reduced them to mere chemical compounds eligible for patents (ibid, p. 409). Disregarding the Supreme Court's insistence on invention rather than discovery, this court opened the doors for patents on naturally occurring genes. This move that resulted in "more than three million gene-related patents" applied for in the next ten years, "several thousand" of which the USPTO approved (ibid, p. 409). Clearly, the Court of Appeals had different ideas than the Supreme Court and did not consider invention a necessary component of patent eligibility. This attitude foreshadows the Australian court decisions regarding Myriad Genetics, and *Chakrabaty* would earn a mention in the reasoning of those decisions.

II. The Origins of the Myriad Genetics Case in the U.S. and Abroad.

During this ten-year wave of genetic patent applications, Myriad applied for a patent on BRCA genes in 1994, with an update to clarify the gene sequence in 1995 (Bosch, 2004, p. 1780). Published research from the University of California, Berkeley in 1990 had revealed "the general location of a gene linked to breast cancer" (Patent Act of 1952, 2013, p. 388). Mary Claire King led the UC team which announced their findings at the American Society of Human Genetics Meeting. Though the team identified the gene BRCA1 "on chromosome 17 through a technique called linkage analysis," researchers from the United Kingdom, France, Belgium, the Netherlands, and Canada all collaborated in attempts to map BRCA1 and BRCA2 (Gold, 2010).

Following this announcement, Mark Skolnick of the University of Utah's Centre for Genetic Epidemiology, a competing laboratory, spun off Myriad Genetics from his group in 1991 to obtain venture capital for this line of research (ibid, 2010). Myriad Genetics soon isolated BRCA1 and BRCA2. Next, they invented clinical testing methods to identify mutations in the genes relating to increased risk for breast and ovarian cancer (Patent Act of 1952, 2013, p. 388). Myriad Genetics sought to patent not only the clinical methods they invented, but the naturally occurring genetic material they discovered.

The USPTO granted Myriad patents covering 47 mutations in the BRCA1 gene in 1997, then five additional patents covering the BRCA1 gene and associated tests, and finally two patents in 1998 "covering methods of detecting BRCA1 mutations and the entire sequence of the BRCA1 gene and tools used" in Myriad's work, the last of which "covered all uses of the BRCA1 gene" (Gold, 2010). The patents positioned Myriad as the only entity with legal rights to isolate the gene itself. And since their testing methods required isolating the gene, they became the only entity with legal rights to test for it, too (Patent Act of 1952, 2013, p. 389).

The patents covering BRCA2 would come later. The Cancer Research Campaign first filed for a patent on BRCA2 in the United Kingdom, having funded research by a UK group of 40 researchers from six countries who published the gene's sequence in *Nature* in December 1995 (Gold, 2010). Just one day before this publication, however, US researchers including Mark Skolnick claimed this work was only a partial sequence and only covered six mutations of BRCA2. Skolnick's group deposited the complete sequence into a database of gene sequences (Gen-Bank), published their findings in *Nature Genetics* in 1996, and filed for US patents—patents issued by the USPTO in 1998 and 2000 (ibid, 2010). In the US, Myriad Genetics gained intellectual property control over BRCA1, BRCA2, the methods of their isolation, and the clinical tests based on the isolation.

Despite approval in the U.S., the patents met resistance overseas—not in courts, but at the European Patent Office (EPO). The EPO had granted three patents to Myriad in January 2001, but "several European research centres, along with other organizations and the European Parliament, filed a joint opposition to the patent in October 2001" (Bosch, 2004, p. 1780). The conflict stemmed not from the debate over invention versus discovery but from Myriad's denial of licenses to research the genes, and its refusal to let any laboratories but its own test DNA samples using its technology (ibid, p. 1780). The opposition called this an "abusive monopoly," and the EPO revoked the patent on May 18, 2004 (ibid, p. 1780). The revoked patent covered the diagnostic test, though the Technical Board of Appeal subsequently limited the scope of the patents on the mutations of the BRCA1 gene in 2005, and the Board greatly limited the patent over BRCA2 that year as well (Gold, 2010). The EPO did not invalidate all of Myriad Genetics' BRCA-related patents, but they greatly limited the scope of the material and testing processes involved.

Myriad Genetics also pursued patent control and licensing arrangements in Canada, but the full extent of the Canadian campaign exceeds the scope of this paper. Briefly, the Canadian province of Ontario supported local BRCA testing without regard to Myriad's patenting attempts in Canada, resulting in a highly charged political situation. At one point, the US made threats of trade sanctions against Canada. But after years of posturing, committee reviews, inflammatory letters, political spectacle, and debate, Myriad "decided to give up on the Canadian market" when they could not bully Canada into enforcing the patents (ibid, 2010). Myriad's failure to force total control over BRCA genes and testing in the European Union and Canada foreshadowed its eventual defeat in the U.S. Supreme Court.

III. The Myriad Genetics Case in the U.S.

In the U.S., opposition began in 2009 when the American Civil Liberties Union (ACLU) and the Public Patent Foundation called the constitutionality of the patents into question, filing suit against Myriad Genetics and the USPTO (Victory for Genes, 2013, p. 792). The ACLU was joined in this effort by "six nonprofit organizations that engage in research and advocacy, eight university-affiliated scientists whose work was impeded by

Myriad's patents, and six individuals who were unable to obtain desired BRCA screenings because of Myriad's monopoly on testing" (Patent Act of 1952, 2013, p. 389). "The District Court for the Southern District of New York granted summary judgment for the plaintiffs in 2010," ruling against Myriad's patent claims for the composition of the BRCA genes and its testing methods (Cong, 2012, p. 755). The District Court "invalidated seven of Myriad's US patents relating to the BRCA1 and BRCA2 genes and associated genetic tests" (Gold, 2010). The judge in this case, Judge Sweet, referred to the existing Supreme Court decisions regarding naturally occurring biological material and physical phenomena (Patent Act of 1952, 2013, p. 389-90). Judge Sweet also struck down the methods claims covering the processes for clinical testing.

The Court of Appeals, however, upheld the patents, reversing the District Court's decision, and again upheld their own decision in August 2012 after the remand ordered by the Supreme Court (Cong, 2012, p. 755). The remand order from the Supreme Court considered its recent decision in *Mayo Collaborative Services v. Prometheus Laboratories, Inc.* "Prometheus, having patented a method of adjusting dosages based on patients' biological response" had sued Mayo Collaborative Services "which had developed a similar test" (Supreme Court Orders, 2012, p. 26). In *Prometheus*, the Supreme Court unanimously found the method in question for determining dosages merely described natural laws, and Justice Breyer made it clear the court believed "granting monopolies over laws of nature through patents would impede future research rather than promote innovation" (Patent Act of 1952, 2013, p. 390). The court ruled in favor of Mayo.

The Circuit Court, ordered to reconsider their decision in this light, still did not agree. In terms of discovery versus invention, the Circuit Court's majority asserted that although the DNA in question occurred naturally, the process of cleaving the DNA and isolating it led to "distinctive chemical composition" that rendered it patent-eligible (Cong, 2012, p. 756). Specifically, the Circuit Court referred to the *Chakrabaty* decision's emphasis on biological material with characteristics different from those occurring in nature. The differing characteristic in *Myriad* was that the isolated BRCA genes lacked introns in their molecules, something they had in their naturally occurring forms, and this lack made them "especially distinctive" (Patent Act of 1952, 2013, p. 391). Judge Lourie's opinion for the majority argued that the genes in question were distinctly different from naturally occurring ones due to their separation from the larger DNA molecule in the isolation process (ibid, p. 391). The Australian courts would later favor this rationale.

While the Supreme Court reached a unanimous decision in *Mayo*, the Circuit Court found itself split on the matter (Rogers, 2013, p. 436). The dissenting opinion argued nothing about the isolation process for BRCA changed the "structure or function of naturally occurring genes," thus invalidating claims of invention and rendering the genes ineligible for patenting (Cong, 2012, p. 756). Judge Bryson's dissenting opinion argued merely separating a component of the larger DNA molecule did not render it any more eligible than a kidney could become patent-eligible upon removal from the human body, or a mineral could become patent-eligible simply because someone extracted it from the earth (Patent Act of 1952, 2013, p. 392). Despite this straightforward, common-sense reasoning, the other Circuit Court judges outvoted Judge Bryson two-to-one. The Circuit Court, in failing to acknowledge that "isolated DNA segments have the identical nucleotide sequence and the same function as native DNA" and lack both the "marked changes required under *Chakrabaty*" and the "inventive step required under *Prometheus*," disregarded "150 years of Supreme Court cases that physical phenomena found in nature and the laws of nature are not patentable subject matter" (Rogers, 2013, p. 434).

Upon the failure of this remand to invalidate the patents, the ACLU petitioned the Supreme Court to take up the case. The court "held that isolated DNA molecules are not patent eligible" and "rejected the Federal Circuit's contention that the chemical changes created during the isolation process made the molecules distinctive" (Patent Act of 1952, 2013, p. 393). The court, consistent with its historical decisions, ruled the BRCA genes "are a product of nature and therefore ineligible for patenting" (Myriad Diagnostic Concerns, 2013, p. 571). This decision was unanimous. It marked the "first time that the US Supreme Court has invalidated a human gene" patent (Victory for Genes, 2013, p. 792).

IV. The Origins of the Myriad Genetics Case in Australia.

The story of Myriad Genetics' patent litigation did not end with the U.S. Supreme Court's decision. It continued in Australia. But before the matter came to court, some interesting things happened with the Australian licensee of the BRCA patents: Genetic Technologies, Ltd (GTG). Myriad Genetics had licensed the BRCA test to GTG "because GTG was pursuing Myriad for patent infringement," and the patent conflict between the companies resolved in each gaining licensing rights to the other's DNA patents (Gold, 2010). Things became complicated in 2007 when Dr. Merv Jacobson, CEO and co-founder of GTG and its largest shareholder, retired. As reported in *Australian Life Scientist*, Jacobson, who would maintain a position as a non-executive director, had preferred not enforcing the company's patent rights on BRCA; instead, he called BRCA testing "GTG's gift to Australia" (O'Neill, 2009).

New CEO Michael Ohanessian decided to change this relaxed policy, a move that would mean public laboratories would "no longer be permitted to perform commercial testing on [their] patients for mutations of the genes," although the change would not block their ability to continue research on the genes (O'Neill, 2009). Dr. Jacobson objected so vehemently that he announced he would seek a resolution to remove Ohanessian and four other directors, the chairman, and three non-executive directors. The effects of this announcement included GTG's requesting the Australian Stock Exchange "halt trading of its shares" (ibid). The company backed down from its threat of enforcing "its patent rights against laboratories offering BRCA testing" in October 2008 (Cook-Deegan, 2014). Ohanessian was eventually deposed as CEO as a result of this conflict, though Dr. Jacobson also resigned soon after (O'Neill, 2009).

The conflict spurred the Australian Senate to hold "a series of hearings, and a bill proscribing DNA sequence patents was proposed, but the new government opposed it, and it lapsed" (Cook-Deegan, 2014). GTG thus enjoyed a position of benevolent power, unthreatened by any new governmental legislation regarding DNA sequences. The difference between the Australian situation and the cases in Europe, Canada, and America lies in the good will of Dr. Jacobson at GTG which could not be more different than the heavy-handed approach Myriad Genetics took to other international markets.

Dr. Jacobson, quoted in *Australian Life Scientist*, explained his position on not enforcing GTG's BRCA testing patents. Dr. Jacobson noted that government laboratories, out of fear of patent enforcement from Myriad Genetics, had begun BRCA testing but not invested in it enough to make it a timely process, and "some women were waiting up to two years, which would put them at risk of developing cancers as they waited." Because GTG won "exclusive rights to perform BRCA testing in Australia and New Zealand," they "set up a state-of-the-art laboratory, at least as good as Myriad's, that would perform BRCA testing accurately, and in much less time." The GTG labs eventually reduced the testing time to "two months" and even "as little as four weeks." Motivated to create a "socially responsible strategy," Jacobson asserted that GTG was not "Myriad's policemen" and did not obtain the patent rights "to beat up other testing laboratories... If people wanted to do BRCA testing themselves, they were free to do so, but if they wanted our help, they had that too" (O'Neill, 2009).

Despite these statements of good will from Dr. Jacobson, the conflict makes it clear that if Genetic Technologies had wanted to enforce its patents, it had the legal right to do so—a legal right that covered both private, potential competitors and public, governmental health facilities. GTG's benevolence stemmed from the humanitarian philosophy of just one doctor, and policy could easily go the other way once he retired or moved on. This is why, in 2010, the BRCA patents entered litigation in Australian courts. It was not, as in the case of the European Patent Office, that Myriad Genetics created an abusive monopoly. It was merely the threat that such a state would come to pass. This is why Paul Grogan, the Director of Advocacy at Cancer Council Australia, would tell the Australian press, "In 2008, Australian women were only protected from an attempted commercial monopoly over the BRCA1 and BRCA2 tests because the company that threatened to take those tests away from public laboratories withdrew its patent claims voluntarily... There was nothing in the law to protect healthcare customers" (Corderoy, 2014). These healthcare customers began the Australian litigation.

V. The Decisions in the Myriad Case in Australia.

The organization Cancer Voices of Australia, along with cancer survivor Yvonne D'Arcy of Brisbane represented by the law firm of Maurice Blackburn, filed suit against Myriad and GTG in 2010 (Guardian, 2014). The case entered the Federal Court of Australia in Sydney, Judge Nicholas presiding (Conley, 2010). Judge Nicholas issued a decision on February 15, 2013 in favor of Myriad and GTG, dismissing all charges (Cancer Voices, 2013, p. 39). An appeals court subsequently heard the case. On September 5, 2014, its panel of five judges unanimously ruled to uphold Judge Nicholas' decision (Cook-Deegan, 2014). The appeals court—the Federal Court of Australia, New South Wales District Registry, General Division—after a lengthy discussion recapitulating the scientific and precedent reasoning of the previous court, dismissed the appeal (D'Arcy, 2014, p. 3). At the time of this paper, the case may still be appealed at one final level—the Australian High Court (Masnick, 2014). Though it may be too early to close the book and draw conclusions about the state of genetic patents in Australia, examining of the reasoning of these two Australian Federal Courts is worthwhile.

As with many of the earlier cases discussed here, Judge Nicholas examined the difference between invention and discovery. He explains, after a lengthy lesson on the fundamentals of DNA and genetic science, the reasoning behind determining "whether isolation of naturally occurring DNA and RNA results in an artificial state of affairs with a discernible effect—whether claims to isolated DNA and RNA are to a 'mere discovery' and therefore not patentable—whether claims to isolated DNA and RNA are to a 'product of nature' and therefore not patentable" (Cancer Voices, 2013). Despite the weight other courts have given to the difference between discovery and invention, the appeals court in Australia found this subject of little concern in their decision. As Dr. Robert Cook-Deegan explained, the legal reasoning of the appeals court:

> "clearly states that a distinction between invention and discovery is not a fruitful conceptual framework for patent law, and quite explicitly rejects the U.S. Supreme Court's arguments in *AMP v Myriad*. The opinion lauds Judge Lourie of the U.S. Court of Appeals for the Federal Circuit, who upheld Myriad's claims on isolated DNA molecules in two majority opinions that were unanimously reversed by the U.S. Supreme Court" (Cook-Deegan, 2014).

Dr. Cook-Deegan may be overstating the appeals court's disregard for the concept of invention versus discovery, though. Paragraphs 110-115 in the decision directly address discovery and invention, cite Australian cases going back to 1903 as precedent, and mention the U.S. cases of *Funk Bros.* and *Chakrabaty* (D'Arcy, 2014, 23-5). The court in this case, however, targeted terms more widely argued in Australian patent law; specifically "artificially created state of affairs" and "matter of manufacture," both terms somewhat unfamiliar in the U.S. but important legal concepts in Australia.

As to whether or not a manufactured item was a "product of nature" and whether or not a microorganism would be "markedly different from something that already exists in nature," the court reasoned "there was no requirement" for determining these things in Australian patent law, based on the precedents (ibid, p. 24). The court examined precedent that "invention may consist of using the material or some new adaptation of it so as to serve the new purpose. If the new use consists in taking advantage of a hitherto unknown or unsuspected property, there may be invention" (ibid, p. 24). The court determined it is "only necessary to show one inventive step in the advance made beyond the prior limits of the relevant art" (ibid, p. 25). In other words, within the context of Australian patent law, invention can mean finding a new use for an old thing, or taking previous uses and advancing them one more step.

This argument about the nature of invention and its relevance to intellectual property and patent rights is nothing new, but neither is it without criticism. The advancement of science and invention relies on methods, equipment, and knowledge of previous workers, researchers, and institutions. In the context of developing new medicines and medical treatments, "the intellectual labor that went into the drug design process did not occur from first principles; rather, in every case, the inventor's thought process was critically shaped by the cumulative insights of his or her predecessors" (Shah, p. 844). This argument does not deny the continual process of invention; rather, it denies the wisdom of granting exclusive patent control to persons, corporations, or institutions who, having stood on the shoulders of giants, now presume to extend unilateral control over products and processes that utterly depend on prior work for their existence.

Wisdom, however, did not concern the Australian appeals court, and it said so:

"This case is not about the wisdom of the patent system. It is about the application of Australian patent law, as set out in the Act and as developed by the courts since the Statute of Monopolies. It is not about whether, for policy or moral or social reasons, patents for gene sequences should be excluded from patentability. ...It is not a matter for the court, but for Parliament to decide. Parliament has considered the question of the patentability of gene sequences and has chosen not to exclude them but to make amendments to the Act to address, in part, the balance between the benefits of the patent system and the incentive thereby created, and the restriction on, for example, subsequent research" (D'Arcy, 2014, p. 47).

If neither concern for wisdom, nor the distinction between invention and discovery, nor ethical problems with patenting products of nature informed the thinking of the court, then what did? In a word: isolation. First, based on the testimony of genetic scientists quoted at length in the decision by Judge Nicholas, the court decided the isolated portions of the DNA molecule in Myriad's isolated BRCA material are chemically "different to the gene comprising the nucleic acid sequence as it exists in nature" (ibid, p. 49). Counter arguments from depositions and testimonies cited in the decision assert the genetic information encoded was still the same, and the chemical changes noted by the court merely resulted from the molecule's separation from its natural place in the chain. The Australian court did not find these counter arguments compelling enough to sway its decision. It stands in opposition to the opinion from Supreme Court Justice Clarence Thomas which states "We... hold that genes and the information they encode are not patent eligible... simply because they have been isolated from the surrounding genetic material" (Victory for Genes, 2013, p. 792).

The court further determined "isolation of the nucleic acid also leads to an economically useful result—in this case, the treatment of breast and ovarian cancers" (D'Arcy, 2014, p. 49). Determining the creation of "economically useful results" plays a significant role in Australian patent law. Plus, while the Supreme Court might find a product of nature ineligible for patent, the Australian court found excluding products of nature "is not in accordance with the principles of patent law in Australia and has been specifically rejected as a reason for exclusion in" a precedent-setting case (ibid, p. 50).

This precedent comes from 1959's *National Research Development Corporation v Commissioner of Patents* which "requires that an invention apply to an 'artificially created state of affairs'" (Cook-Deegan, 2014). As Dr. Robert Cook-Deegan explained, "this criterion in effect means that if 'we did it in our lab' it will clear the threshold for patent eligibility. Given this precedent, the Federal Court's ruling is sensible" (ibid, 2014). The genetic material isolated in Myriad Genetics' processes "has resulted in an artificially created state of affairs for economic benefit," and therefore "is properly the subject of letters patent" that meets the requirements of section 18(1) of Australia's Patent Acts 1990 (D'Arcy, 2014, p. 50).

Thus, the two Australian courts decided in favor of the patent-eligibility of Myriad's clinical testing processes and the piece of genetic material the tests isolate from human DNA, given the slight chemical change (absence of introns) that happens in the isolation process. The Australian courts believe this subtle distinction does not threaten to extend patent control to the human genome itself either in part or in whole. As Judge Nicholas noted in his original decision,

> "There is no doubt that naturally occurring DNA and RNA as they exist inside the cells of the human body cannot be the subject of a valid patent. However, the disputed claims do not cover naturally occurring DNA and RNA as they exist inside such cells. The disputed claims extend only to naturally occurring DNA and RNA which have been extracted from cells obtained from the human body and purged of other biological materials with which they were associated" (Cancer Voices, 2013, p. 38-9).

Dr. Cook-Deegan argued this rationale about isolation, however, is a "lawyer's trick" that creates patent infringement on the part of anyone attempting to analyze DNA molecules containing the BRCA sequences; and, the imprecise nature of defining isolated genetic material—as opposed to the same material in its original place in the DNA molecule—will block any researcher's ability to access, understand, or experiment on these cancer-associated mutations without being subject to potential litigation (Cook-Deegan, 2014). Myriad's patent claims include "broadest method claims" giving them "exclusive rights to any way of comparing the DNA sequence from a sample to the reference sequence of the BRCA1 and BRCA2 genes disclosed in

Myriad's patents" (Cook-Deegan, 2013, p. 298). This means the patents, as upheld by the Australian case, at least, extend to merely comparing a DNA sample to the known (and naturally occurring) BRCA sequences. In other words, a public health facility or private laboratory cannot even compare a sample to a piece of discovered human DNA without infringing the patent. Or, to put it in simplest terms: *Do not even look at it*. It is difficult to imagine how such utter control over genetic research activities can possibly benefit innovation, despite proponents of the Australia decision rallying around the judgment as a victory for medical and genetic innovation.

VI. Conclusion.

These concerns may well be met and resolved in the Australian High Court, or they may not. Either way, the story will not end there. Each nation has its own patent laws. Each nation potentially faces this same time-consuming and costly journey through the judicial system to arrive at its own conclusions. Australia and the U.S. have cooperated extensively on creating mutual trade agreements to cover intellectual property rights and patent rights. But their opposing decisions on the Myriad Genetics cases demonstrate patent laws on biological materials and the human genome have not yet reached the level of international standardization aimed for by instruments like the World Trade Organization's TRIPS and TRIPS-plus agreements. If such a standard already existed, such as ones developing for pharmaceutical products, software, and other forms of intellectual property, the U.S. Supreme Court and the Federal Court of Australia would not find themselves so diametrically opposed on such a fundamental concern.

Patents, as a means of claiming property rights to produce financial gain, involve the economic incentives for knowledge production. Is patent protection of knowledge necessary to drive the innovation required for growth and technological advancement in today's information society? No clear consensus exists. As one Australian patent lawyer said in response to the

September ruling by the appeals court, "This decision is also certainly not going to stifle research and innovation in this field; in fact, I wonder if we will see more U.S. companies starting to try to commercialise things here" (Corderoy, 2014). This echoes a belief held by some in the U.S. that the Supreme Court's ruling is "the latest of a series of reverses to the intellectual property (IP) foundations needed to support innovative diagnostic enterprises" (Myriad Diagnostic Concerns, 2013, p. 571).

Such arguments miss the finer point: the distinction between patenting innovative processes for researching genetic material and clinically testing it, versus patenting the genetic material itself. This is the wisdom in Judge Bryson's opinion at the U.S. Circuit Court level. Judge Bryson understood that innovation and invention reside in new ways of doing things, new technologies, new processes and methods, new equipment and products. These are the things that patents were meant to cover, not the human genome, and not naturally occurring phenomenon. Judge Bryson understood this point, the Supreme Court came to understand it, and the European Patent Office and Canada also understood it. All of them have invalidated, ignored, or severely restricted the kind of patent rights Myriad Genetics and its licensees have tried so vigorously to assert for more than a decade now in their nations.

One might easily suspect the Australian courts understood the distinction as well, but brushed it aside to create a climate where U.S. corporations would feel encouraged to bring new businesses and new streams of revenue to their nation. As one of the leading proponents of international trade agreements governing intellectual property rights, Australia may well set the tone of patent legislation being designed in developing nations seeking to become compliant with TRIPS and join the World Trade Organization. Other nations may look to them as a role model for creating patent laws concerning human genetic material based not on reality or science or common sense, but purely on the desire to attract multinational corporations into doing business in their country. The case of Myriad Genetics has been long and complex. But in today's era of globalization, it is far from over.

References

Association for Molecular Pathology v. Myriad Genetics, Inc. (2013, June 13). *United States Supreme Court*. Full syllabus, opinion, and concurrence: http://supreme.justia.com/cases/federal/us/569/12-398/

"Australian federal court rules isolated genetic material can be patented." (2014, September 4). *The Guardian*. http://www.theguardian.com/world/2014/sep/05/court-rules-breast-cancer-gene-brca1-patented-australia

Bosch, Xavier. (2004, May 29). "Myriad loses rights to breast cancer gene patent." *Lancet, 363*(9423), 1780-1780.

Cancer Voices Australia v. Myriad Genetics Inc [2013] FCA 65. (2013, February 15). *Federal Court of Australia*. Full text including corrigendum added 25 February: http://www.judgments.fedcourt.gov.au/judgments/Judgments/fca/single/2013/2013fca0065

Cong Yao. (2012). "Federal circuit holds isolated DNA is patent-eligible—Association for Molecular Pathology v. United States Patent and Trademark Office (Myriad III)." *American Journal of Law & Medicine, (38)*4, 755-757.

Conley, John. (2010, June 21). "Myriad gene patent litigation goes down under." *Genomics Law Report*. http://www.genomicslawreport.com/index.php/2010/06/21/myriad-litigation-goes-down-under/

Cook-Deegan, Robert. (2014, September 30). "Australian appeals court upholds patents on isolated BRCA1 DNA." *Genomics Law Report*. http://www.genomicslawreport.com/index.php/2014/09/30/australian-appeals-court-upholds-patents-on-isolated-brca1-dna/#more-13366

Cook-Deegan, Robert. (2013, August 20). "Are human genes patentable?" *Annals of Internal Medicine, 159*(4), 298-300.

Corderoy, Amy. (2014, September 5). "Mutation of breast cancer gene can be patented, says Federal Court." *The Sydney Morning Herald.*
http://www.smh.com.au/national/health/mutation-of-breast-cancer-gene-can-be-patented-says-federal-court-20140905-10ckfp.html

D'Arcy v. Myriad Genetics Inc [2014] FCAFC 115 (2014, September 5). *Federal Court of Australia.*
http://www.austlii.edu.au/au/cases/cth/FCAFC/2014/115.html

Gold, Richard, Carbone, Julia. (2010, April). "Myriad Genetics: In the eye of the policy storm." *Genetics in Medicine, 12*(4) Suppl., S39-S70. doi:10.1097/GIM.0b013e3181d72661
http://www.nature.com/gim/journal/v12/n1s/full/gim2010142a.html

Leal, R. (2014, Spring). "The next step in gene patents: Association for Molecular Pathology v. Myriad Genetics." *Journal of Art, Technology & Intellectual Property Law, 24*(2), 403-423.

Masnick, Mike. (2014, September 9). "Australian court disagrees with US: Claim genes are totally patentable." *TechDirt.*
https://www.techdirt.com/articles/20140905/16275828438/australian-court-disagrees-with-us-claim-genes-are-totally-patentable.shtml

"Myriad diagnostic concerns." [Editorial]. (2013, July). *Nature Biotechnology, 31*(7), 571. doi:10.1038/nbt.2638

O'Neill, Graeme. (2009, April 3). "Jacobson speaks: Genetic Technologies and BRCA testing." *Australian Life Scientist.*
http://lifescientist.com.au/content/molecular-

biology/article/jacobson-speaks-genetic-technologies-and-brca-testing-1127244197

"Patent Act of 1952—Patentable Subject Matter—Ass'n for Molecular Pathology v. Myriad Genetics, Inc. (2013, November)." *Harvard Law Review*, 127(1), 388-407.

Rogers, Douglas L. (2013). "After Prometheus, are human genes patentable subject matter?" *Duke Law & Technology Review*, 11(2), 434-508.

Shah, A. K., Warsh, J., Kesselheim, A. (2013, Winter). "The ethics of intellectual property rights in an era of globalization." *Journal of Law, Medicine & Ethics*, 41(4), 841-851. doi:10.1111/jlme.12094

"Supreme Court orders new review of Myriad gene patents." (2012, April/May). *GeneWatch*, 25(3), 26.

"A Victory for Genes." [Editorial]. (2013, July). *Nature Medicine*, 19(7), 792. doi:10.1038/nm.3279

8

Patents and Public Health in the Age of TRIPS:
Why the Future Depends on Connecting Patent Offices with Public Health Agencies

Abstract

Abstract

Conflicts between public health and the commercial interests of multinational pharmaceutical companies have come to the forefront of TRIPS criticism in light of recent health crises, including viral outbreaks and HIV. Multinational pharmaceutical companies played a significant role in creating TRIPS. They use its provisions to apply for patents in developing nations. The patents give them legal rights to control the supply of that medicine in that country, something public health agencies often confront only after it is too late. Ironically, TRIPS regulations do contain many provisions that developing nations could invoke to protect public health, provisions called flexibilities. However, these flexibilities may never make it into the country's legislation due to both a lack of resources in developing nations and pressure on patent offices to generate revenue by approving applications. Political pressures coerce nations to create TRIPS-based regulation granting pharmaceutical companies far more control than the nation needs to. In this high-powered, high-pressure global arena of TRIPS legislation, public health agencies desperately need to connect with patent offices to take a more influential role in developing and enforcing TRIPS regulations for their country. Administrative challenges faced by the patent offices also deserve attention, for the resources at the patent office in a developing nation do not equal those of developed nations. Therefore, the future of public health depends on the ability of patent offices around the world to achieve parity with the systems and resources of developed nations, and to connect in meaningful ways with public health agencies to fully evaluate the health implications of TRIPS legislation.

Keywords: Agreement on Trade-Related Aspects of Intellectual Property Rights, Doha Declaration, ethics, flexibilities, HIV/AIDS, intellectual property, international trade agreement, medicine, multinational pharmaceutical company, patent, patent office, pharmaceuticals, public administration, public health, TRIPS, TRIPS-plus, World Trade Organization.

I. Medicine as Intellectual Property.

The acronym TRIPS refers to an international trade agreement called the Agreement on Trade-Related Aspects of Intellectual Property Rights. It covers "patents, copyrights, trademarks, industrial design, and trade secrets" (Goodwin, 2008, p. 570). Led by the United States, the European Union, and Japan, a coalition of developed nations created TRIPS in 1994. "Intense lobbying by large multinationals including Pfizer, IBM, and Monsanto" helped shape the U.S. position on the agreement which focused on pharmaceuticals, software, agriculture, and entertainment products (Halbert, 2005). The U.S. during the Clinton Administration identified its copyright-based industries as its major exports and revenue generators, moving away from an earlier era of supremacy in manufacturing (Sum, 2003, p. 377). Given this period of history saw the rise of the North American Free Trade Agreement (NAFTA) and concerns over manufacturing jobs moving to other countries with cheaper labor, this historical shift to focusing on intellectual property should come as no surprise. The creation of TRIPS coincides with the creation of the World Trade Organization (WTO) in 1995 (Sum, 2003, p. 378). Ratifying the TRIPS agreement is now a condition for a nation to belong to the WTO and enjoy the free-trade benefits of membership. TRIPS aims to standardize protection of intellectual property rights among all WTO member nations (Shah p. 841).

What is intellectual property? The World Intellectual Property Organization (WIPO) defines intellectual property as "creations of the mind, such as inventions; literary and artistic works; designs; and symbols, names and images used in commerce" (WIPO, 2014). Though somewhat vague, this definition appears more concrete than some. Even in college classrooms today, students may learn that intellectual property "is the product of your research, hard work, and imagination" (Lanning, 2012, p.82). But such vague definitions raise many questions. If a man works hard to dig a ditch, is the ditch a form of intellectual property? Few would argue in favor of that proposition, even if the man had to perform research about where to dig and what tools to use. Intellectual property must be somehow distinguishable from physical, tangible property. The WIPO definition comes closest to defining where the difference lies and what the term covers. Even so, exactly what constitutes intellectual property, and to what extent anyone owns it, remains a point of contention.

Members of the WTO find themselves, under TRIPS, obliged to issue patents to protect pharmaceuticals as simply another form of property, like other forms of technology (Walker, 2001, p. 112). The inclusion of medicines in TRIPS as just another form of intellectual property—like a business logo, a fictional character, or even this essay—has caused the most widespread criticism and dispute of TRIPS. While other technologies such as software have given rise to disputes as well, access to medicine by the sick and poor in developing nations has caused the most outspoken response to TRIPS by governments, academics, and human rights groups around the world.

In terms of medicine, the claim that a newly synthesized medicine should become intellectual property remains open to debate. From the methods and equipment used in the research and development of the medicine to the previous research which provided a basis for it, the creation of a new medicine relies on the prior work of others. "The intellectual labor that went into the drug design process did not occur from first principles; rather, in every case, the inventor's thought process was critically shaped by the cumulative insights of his or her predecessors" (Shah, p. 844). To arrive at the final step and then claim total ownership appears to ignore history and the work of others.

In fact, the notion that property rights can apply to any idea at all remains open to debate. Taking another person's car, or house, or tools, or any real, physical object deprives the person of their use. But, recognizing a good idea and using it for oneself does not impede the originator's use of that same idea (Hilton, 2005, p. 72). Many people can enjoy the use of a good idea without detracting from any other person's use of that idea. While shoelaces may be considered a person's property, it would seem ridiculous to patent the idea of tying one's shoelaces to demand payments from every person who ties their shoelaces in the future. Many TRIPS-related agreements accomplish just that, only in terms of medicine. They even cover any future uses one might discover for the medicines, as if one could also patent every future use people might later invent for shoelaces beyond affixing shoes to one's feet.

The application of intellectual property law to medicines under TRIPS has caused conflict. The key disputes have come from nations affected by viral outbreaks, especially HIV/AIDS, which found themselves at the economic mercy of the patent holders of the necessary medicines. Multinational pharmaceutical companies hold these patents, and the disputes brought against them have led to reinterpretations and evaluations of TRIPS. This essay will take a closer look at specific cases, their disputes, and their consequences.

II. Commercial Interest versus Public Health.

Multinational pharmaceutical companies led by interests in the U.S., the European Union, and Japan played a significant role in defining how TRIPS treats patents (Halbert, 2005). Prior to TRIPS, patent offices in some developing countries would not patent pharmaceuticals in order to keep down the cost of medicine, or they only allowed patents on the "process" of creating the medicine—not the product itself (Van Puymbroeck, 2010, p. 525). HIV/AIDS medicines can be relatively inexpensive to produce, but, under TRIPS, the multinational pharmaceutical corporations who hold the patents can drive the purchase price up to where developing nations cannot readily afford it. Rather than "free trade," this creates artificial scarcity.

However, TRIPS and its subsequent interpretations have shown some protections for public health. Compulsory licenses allow the use of patented medicines by the public health sector and circumvent the standard licensing regulations to deal with emergencies (ibid, p. 525). These licenses are issued under judicial and administrative review and must be for government use only, not for private gain.

"International political pressure" forced the WTO to reconsider TRIPS in light of the growing spread of HIV/AIDS in developing countries and specifically in Africa (Halbert, 2005). This resulted in the Doha Declaration, which sought to clarify that nothing about TRIPS—regardless of its language—should be construed as constraining governments from taking measures to protect public health (Van Puymbroeck, 2010, p. 526). Formally known as the Declaration on the TRIPS Agreement and Public Health, this 2001 document from the WTO states that "the TRIPS agreement does not and should not prevent members from taking measures to protect public health," and that the interpretation and implementation of TRIPS should support "WTO members' right to protect public health and, in particular, to promote access to medicines for all" (Kobori, 2002, p. 11).

Multinational pharmaceutical corporations such as GlaxoSmithKline voice opposition to the government-forced compulsory licenses mandated during public health crises. These compulsory licenses stifle innovation, according to the Pharmaceutical Research and Manufacturers of America (PhrMA) (Van Puymbroeck, 2010, p. 525). However, counter arguments include criticisms that the TRIPS system has also failed to innovate medicines for developing countries. The World Health Organization's 2006 report, issued by its Commission on Innovation, Intellectual Property, and Public Health, found that when people and nations are too poor to purchase medicines for diseases that are killing millions of people, patents do not encourage research, development, and innovations to bring new medicines to that market (Outterson, 2008, p. 279). If a country has no money for research and development, this report proposes, then it will fail to innovate its own medicines for its own health crises. And if it has no money, such a country offers no financial incentive to more wealthy nations to develop and sell medicines to it. After all, few companies innovate products for people who cannot pay for them. A market must exist for innovations to arise from profit motives, and the infrastructure must exist to make innovation possible.

Another argument supporting the contentions of the pharmaceutical companies relates to their ability to recoup the cost of bringing the medicines to market. However, sales of medicines in developed countries, whose wealthier populations can generally afford higher-priced medicines, compensate for lower revenues from developing nations (Walker, 2001, p. 111). Few would argue the corporations in question should lose money to develop medicines, but inflating prices in developing nations is not the only solution available to them. Moreover, developing nations only generate a relatively small amount of profits for pharmaceutical companies compared to developed nations. As of 2008, eighty to ninety percent of global sales of patented medicines came from the thirty wealthiest nations in the Organization for Economic Cooperation and Development, suggesting that if "developing countries cannot currently afford the drugs... pharmaceutical companies are not foregoing any revenue by providing the drugs at generic prices" (Goodwin, 2008, p. 576).

Is it really the high cost of medicines that prevents them from reaching the poor people who need them most? The patent lawyers for these pharmaceutical companies have issued statements that lack of money and infrastructure in developing countries, not the patents, interfere with distribution of medicine (Van Puymbroeck, 2010, p. 525). But UNAIDS, the United Nations organization that studies and treats HIV/AIDS worldwide, found the "patents that allow exclusive control over the manufacture, import, and sale" do play a role in creating high prices for treatments, and these high prices necessarily restrict the poor's access to the medicines (Walker, 2001, p. 110). The World Health Organization found high cost presented "one of the major obstacles to providing access to essential medications in developing countries," and the U.S. Government Accountability Office notes that developing nations may "spend as much as seventy percent of their health care budgets on medication" compared to fifteen percent or less in developed nations

(Goodwin, 2008, p. 570). Few can doubt the patents relate to high costs, and high costs relate to a lack of access to the medicines in developing nations.

However, patents and high cost cannot unilaterally bear the blame for the problems in distributing medicines to the sick and the poor in developing nations. In developing nations, many people live far away from hospitals, society lacks sufficient training for doctors, and governments may be corrupt and dysfunctional—all of which contributes to a lack of access to even the inexpensive medicines (Dutfield, 2008, p. 108). The Center for International Development surveyed fifty-three countries in Africa to identify where patents existed for fifteen antiretroviral medicines used in HIV/AIDS treatment. Published in the *Journal of the American Medical Association* in 2001, the survey found that few of the countries had issued patent protection for these medicines, and the existing patents mostly stemmed from three companies: Pfizer, GlaxoSmithKline, and Boehringer Ingelheim (Kobori, 2002, p. 13).

Counterarguments from nongovernmental organizations questioned this survey. They pointed out it ignored many significant products that had, in fact, been patented in those countries, and that surveying only fifteen medicines out of "a potential 795 drugs, or combinations of drugs" gave a woefully inadequate picture of the true situation (ibid, p. 13). It might serve the commercial interest of multinational pharmaceutical corporations to place the blame anywhere but on their revenue-generating patents, but it is true patents are not the only obstacle to distributing medicines in the developing nations of the world. Patents are, however, a contributing factor, and they are one that public administration can address.

Compulsory licenses and the Doha Declaration aside, TRIPS member nations have other flexibilities available to protect public health and set their own standards for what gets patented and what does not (Correa, 2001, p. 79). Why many nations fail to fully utilize these flexibilities will be the subject of later sections of this essay. However, it is worth noting here that TRIPS member nations, as members of the World Trade Organization, enjoy some rights to combat "abuses" of intellectual property control. For example, the Competition Commission of South Africa won licenses for four companies to produce AIDS medicine as recourse to price gouging by GlaxoSmithKline and Boehringer Ingelheim (Van Puymbroeck, 2010, p. 527). The WTO, as both enforcer and evaluator of TRIPS and its disputes, has simultaneously set the stage for these abuses to arise due to commercial interests, and also created the arena in which they may be resolved in favor of public health.

The Doha Declaration and the TRIPS flexibilities gave rise to Canada's 2005 adoption of the Jean Chretién Pledge to Africa, an amendment to Canada's patent laws now known as Canada's Access to Medicines Regime (CAMR) (Goodwin, 2008, p. 569). The Doha Declaration ordered the TRIPS Council to remedy the restrictions that TRIPS Article 31 placed on governments desiring to apply for compulsory licenses to distribute patented medicines during health crises. Article 31 limited governments to medicines their domestic markets could supply, something that proved a major obstacle in nations lacking research and development facilities and funding to even have such domestic market. The TRIPS Council created a remedy in Paragraph 6 which dealt with the export of patented medicines to countries who faced challenges creating their own medicines domestically. Canada "became the first country to authorize the manufacture of generic medications under the Paragraph 6 Division when it authorized Apotex, Inc. to manufacture 260,000 packs of TriAvir (in generic form, ApoTriavir,) an HIV/AIDS medication, for export to Rwanda" (ibid, p. 569).

The Canadian example demonstrates the potential for public administrators to bring public health to the forefront when creating or modifying their patent laws. Certainly the commercial interest of the authorized manufacturer plays a role, but CAMR shows a potential to break the stranglehold patent-holding multinationals exert on a developing nations' government. As the patent office section of this paper will discuss, multinational pharmaceutical companies have often blocked a government's ability to manufacture and distribute generic versions of

132 | Matthew Howard

HIV/AIDS medicines. Removing these blocks can mean a lengthy and costly legal battle for the affected nation. CAMR shows one way out of this trap: the export of generic medicines by a more developed nation to a less developed one. Norway, for example, soon followed Canada's lead by amending their patent laws governing compulsory licenses in such a way that "the King may by regulations prescribe rules that deviate from" only issuing compulsory licenses to supply their own domestic market, and seven other WTO member nations subsequently "amended their patent laws to allow for the export of generic medication under Paragraph 6" (ibid, p.577).

CAMR was not without its criticisms, however, and public administrators should be aware of them. For example, the list of drugs and vaccines covered by CAMR only contained fifty-seven medications, mostly HIV/AIDS related, many of which already had generic competitors or were not covered by patents (Outterson, 2008, p. 282). If the goal was alleviating the lack of access to patented medicines and their generic forms, then Canada's Access to Medicines Regimes may not have taken things far enough.

Furthermore, Canada has a lengthy review process for medicines, and this applies to medicines created for export, not simply their own domestic use (Goodwin, 2008, p. 578). This lengthy review process, combined with a somewhat complex application process for a nation requesting the generic medications, may limit Canada from getting medicines prepared for export in a timely fashion when confronted with a health crisis. Finally, the multinational pharmaceutical companies holding the patents may also have recourse to opposing these measures. Fortunately, for thousands of Rwandans, GlaxoSmithKline did not oppose the distribution of ApoTriavir in this case and also agreed to "waive royalty payments it would otherwise be entitled to under CAMR... on the condition that medication is supplied on a not-for-profit basis" (ibid, p. 575).

The Canadian Access to Medicines Regime, though imperfect, demonstrates how a developed nation can take action, even in this age of TRIPS, to provide assistance to developing nations.

The future of public health depends on this good will, for the inequities in resources, infrastructure, and money between developed and developing nations suggest that developing nations cannot achieve all they need on their own. The governments and governmental agencies of developed nations will need to help less-developed nations by giving priority to their humanitarian and public health concerns. In addition, the patent offices of developed nations will need to bridge the gaps of inequity to help the patent offices and public health agencies in the developing world achieve parity in their systems, resources, and expertise. Many failures of developing nations to adequately address public health under their TRIPS regulations stem from inability to evaluate and administer their regulations and patent offices effectively. The next sections of this essay will examine how these inequities affect, in practical terms, the operations of patent offices around the world and lead to public health crises.

III. The Consequence of Inequities between Nations.

Inequities in wealth and resources between developed and developing nations cause concern that the poorest nations will be exploited by the stronger ones. TRIPS and similar intellectual property controls cause fear their aim is not stimulating innovation but giving the dominant players from developed nations the power to make all human thought and knowledge into commodities, and to profit from this at the expense of nations and peoples (Häyrinen-Alestalo, 2001, p. 207). In the field of public health, this fear takes a specific form. People fear that multinational pharmaceutical companies and their interests in developed nations will use patents to control their medicines. Then, the companies gain a position where they can set any price they choose, and gouge the poorer countries to pay for medicine at artificially high prices. Also, the patents can prevent the use of medicines developed in competing labs independently of the patent-holder. And, the patents can prevent governments from creating and distributing less expensive generic medicines to their people. All these fears have basis in fact, as they have already come to pass.

Critics argue the stronger, more developed nations forced TRIPS on developing nations that did not yet have the infrastructure and resources to be ready for it (Van Puymbroeck, 2010, p. 525). However, the least developed nations had an extended time to adopt TRIPS: as late as 2013 for most of the regulation and until January 1, 2016 for pharmaceutical patents. Despite this extension, countries often find themselves coerced into accepting stricter regulations than the standard TRIPS agreement before gaining entry as a member nation.

Even when nations voluntarily choose to adopt more than the minimum standards of TRIPS, these TRIPS-plus agreements can place more value on intellectual property rights than public health. For example, the Australia-United States Free Trade Agreement (AUFSTA) contained proposed modifications to TRIPS. Critics pointed out that AUFSTA "potentially limits compulsory licensing for 'failure to work,'" and possibly restricts "the opportunity for Australia to rely on the 'flexibility' to implement laws that 'protect public health and nutrition'" (Lawson, 2004, p. 357). AUFSTA also proposed to expressly require patents for "any new uses or methods of using a known product" (ibid, p. 358).

In terms of medicines or medical treatments, this would extend patent control over any new way of using an existing product. This practice resembles patenting aspirin, then patenting its use to relieve headaches, and then separately patenting its use to reduce fever, and insisting on patent protection for every possible use subsequently discovered. Many medicines developed to alleviate depression have shown this ability to be repurposed, for example. Through clinical trials, a number of anti-depressants have also proven effective for smoking cessation, obesity reduction, and other uses (Shah, 2013, p. 846). TRIPS-plus regulations like the ones proposed in Australia would seek to extend intellectual property rights to cover all these new uses. Despite allowing for compulsory licenses in a national emergency, these AUFSTA propositions clearly sought even more restrictive control over the flexibilities and licenses that directly affect public health. They aim to attract foreign investment and technology with stronger intellectual property rights at the expense of protections for public health.

TRIPS has raised concerns that stronger nations have gained the power to monopolize information and innovation at the expense of poorer countries. Developing nations may simply adopt TRIPS without modification, or copy developed nations' intellectual property laws because they lack the resources to draft and evaluate their own effective legislation. In 2005, the World Health Organization reported many developing nations have not taken advantage of the maximum flexibilities allowed under the Doha interpretation. This means that developing nations have not taken full advantage of all the protections available to them.

Why not? They may not have the resources and expertise to do something about it. Complying with TRIPS patent regulations means developing nations bear the cost of catching up with more developed patent offices. Developing nations bear this cost while also bearing the brunt of payments on patents, a cost in the billions of dollars worldwide as money flows from poorer countries to richer ones. Just in the field of software, for example, the organization Free and Open Source Software for Africa calculated that as of 2004, sub-Saharan countries paid "$24 billion each year to (mainly US-based) software companies to secure the use of proprietary products" (May, 2006, p. 123). A <u>full</u> implementation of TRIPS could, by some economists' calculations, result in $40 billion in increased patent payments to the United States, Germany, Japan, France, the United Kingdom, and Switzerland (Van Puymbroeck, 2010, p. 529).

Policy makers need to consider how this economic imbalance determines which companies gain dominance over others and how it affects international trade negotiations. Patent litigation is a costly process that drives out smaller competitors who may have legitimate claims but cannot afford the lengthy trials. Fighting a competitor in court takes money. Even a favorable outcome in a trial can be a pyrrhic victory at best, with court costs and lawyer fees turning into an expense that dwarfs any gains the winning party might have made. In the U.S., many people know how Microsoft squeezed out competitors though patent litigation in the early days of their rise to prominence. On an international level, researchers and companies in poorer countries face the risk of being squeezed out by powerful multinationals in similar disputes. A plea for these nations to settle their disputes in courts really does little to protect their interests.

IV. Problems and Power at the Patent Offices.

For patent offices around the world, the ethical and conceptual concerns raised by TRIPS become practical, administrative concerns. Even before TRIPS, the three major patent offices in the world—the Trilateral of the U.S., Europe, and Japan—had already progressed towards a unified, global system of patent administration. Acting as hubs for patent information, the Trilaterals had improved their data systems for reviewing new applications and searching for prior ones, and then gradually opened these systems for access by other patent offices around the world (Drahos, 2008, p. 155).

But even though the information hub exists, not all the spokes connect to it equally due to their local limitations. In *"Trust Me": Patent Office in Developing Countries*, Peter Drahos writes of his visits to patent offices in the Philippines, Laos, and Indonesia. He found people moving boxes of paper files from one floor to another to make photocopies, five workers sharing a single desktop computer, and whole offices waiting for computers to arrive just so they could get up and running (ibid, p. 159). These examples highlight the inequities in resources between developed and developing nations. Even if the most powerful nations on earth are ready for TRIPS, their less developed neighbors may struggle to achieve an equal footing.

The lack of resources creates opportunities for multinationals to apply for patents in nations which lack the infrastructure to evaluate the potential effects of issuing the patent. For example, registering an HIV treatment in a developing nation might prevent the government from using less expensive generic treatments for major public health crises. This is not a purely hypothetical concern.

In 1998, the patent office in Thailand issued Bristol-Meyers Squibb a patent on Dideoxy Purine Nucleosides, a form of the medicine didanosine. Didanosine is, in simple terms, a medicine used to treat HIV. The World Health Organization includes it on their *List of Essential Medicines* (WHO, 2013, p. 12). The patent protection forced Thailand's Government Pharmaceutical Organization to stop manufacturing their generic version of the medicine. Six years of litigation and campaigning by the government and citizens of Thailand resulted only in Bristol-Meyers Squibb withdrawing the patent. The courts never ruled on it and therefore established no legal precedent to deal with similar patents in the future (Drahos, 2008, p. 166). This case illustrates the pitfalls of pressuring patent offices to handle applications from multinational pharmaceutical companies regardless of their ability to evaluate potential public health concerns.

Yet the local patent offices are not without powers of their own. In fact, they have significant power to affect the course of international trade agreements like TRIPS and even the resulting patent litigation. In the Thailand case, the patent office "came under criticism because it intervened in ways that favoured Bristol-Meyers Squibb" (ibid, p. 167). Why would the patent office try to sway the court case in Bristol-Meyers Squibb's favor? One might suspect pressure to generate revenue. The patent offices collect fees, and a wave of multinational pharmaceuticals registering in Thailand would generate potentially significant revenue.

Local patent offices also play an influential role in negotiating trade agreements like TRIPS and TRIPS-plus. They often provide the negotiating expertise for developing countries which have trade negotiations with more developed countries, especially where intellectual property comes into play. They take an active role in "interpreting, advising, and negotiating standards of patent protection" (ibid, p. 162-3). Patent offices could, if they wished, exercise power protectively by denying patents so their country can reverse-engineer the innovations (ibid, p. 169). But more often than not, to the detriment of public health, the patent office accepts the application fee and issues the patent to the multinational pharmaceutical company.

That local patent offices have a pro-patent bias comes as no surprise. To protect their revenue, they have a financial incentive to oppose any initiatives that question how they issue patents. They gain power to do this because they have access to resources of the patent offices of developed countries, and because their work is so technical that the public cannot easily evaluate it (ibid, p. 163). But financial self-interest alone does not account for all actions of a patent office. The sheer volume of patent applications globally tends to focus the system on issuing patents quickly and efficiently, not necessarily the quality of the results for public health.

Neither the challenges nor the powers of patent offices are clear to public health officials, who often have no interaction with them until after the medical patent becomes a problem. Patent offices do not often connect with the offices of public health in their country. Many health officials have no knowledge of how their local patent offices work or what they currently have for review. Only communication between public health departments and the patent offices during the patent reviews can bridge the gap.

Patent offices enjoy other powers built into the additional flexibilities of TRIPS. They may refuse patents on surgical and diagnostic techniques, therapeutic methods, and any inventions which, when used commercially, would threaten public health. They may also refuse to patent plants and animals.

The patenting of plants and animals was once not possible even in the U.S., owing to a 1948 Supreme Court decision in *Funk Brothers Seed Co. v. Kalo Inoculant Co.* The court ruled that "simply combining several existing species of bacteria into one product was not patentable because all of the components of the invention were known and naturally occurring" (Leal, 2014, p. 407). Subsequent court decisions in the United States overturned this precedent by granting patentability to specific genes and even multicellular organisms (ibid, p. 408).

Now, TRIPS flexibilities allow the courts of other nations to make this decision on their own, rather than merely copy the U.S. This flexibility has more to do with agriculture and genetically modified organisms than medicine; but it affects public health to the extent these living things serve as food for humans and livestock.

A sophisticated understanding of TRIPS and its flexibilities ideally informs a nation's public health agencies about steps they can take to protect the public. An example from India demonstrates that developing nations need not consider sophisticated use of flexibilities a lost cause. Prior to TRIPS, many of the Indian companies developing medicines were not solely profit-driven companies. This did not change despite India's need to pass intellectual property laws that complied with TRIPS to gain membership in the WTO (Bhattacharya, 2008, p. 396). India created a speedy process for applications for compulsory licenses, an administrative move that placed the needs of the sick and the poor above commercial interests in times of public health crises. India's Patent Act, ratified in 2005 as part of their TRIPS-related regulations, took into account the development of HIV/AIDS medicines before joining the WTO, addressing the problem proactively instead of waiting for costly legal disputes or public outcry.

While as imperfect as any of the measures discussed in this essay, the India example suggests that even in the age of TRIPS, public health can play just as important a role as commercial interests in a nation's approach to intellectual property and medicine. Patent offices and public health agencies must fully consider the flexibilities available to them, and look for ways to draft legislation that truly serves the public. TRIPS is heavily skewed in favor of the multinational pharmaceutical companies, but that does not mean a nation must accept exploitation.

Developing nations will need help and support from developed nations to realize this goal effectively. This seems only fair, as the pressure to accept and implement TRIPS comes from those same developed nations that could best help their global neighbors protect their people. In an age of increasingly deadly viral outbreaks and new diseases, the future of public health depends on this helpful and humanitarian approach that prioritizes people over profit, a world view that promotes assistance over exploitation.

V. The Future of Patent Offices and Public Health.

Researchers and administrators face a common problem: understanding the scope and effect of TRIPS requires additional knowledge of international trade agreements that have sought to clarify or expand TRIPS. TRIPS establishes baseline standards; but, many nations have created expanded agreements, often called TRIPS-Plus or TRIPS+.

Consider just a few examples. The 1996 World Intellectual Property Organization Copyright Treaty (WIPO) aimed at reducing circumvention of Digital Rights Management (DRM) protection. In the field of arts and entertainment, broadcasters and webcasters sought rights over their broadcasts by campaigning for a WIPO Broadcasting Treaty in addition to TRIPS regulations. The European Union in 2001 created a Copyright Directive aimed at more enforcement of patent laws than TRIPS provided.

The proliferation of these extended agreements demonstrates the tip of the iceberg of regulations and paperwork someone faces when attempting to learn about TRIPS and its consequences. In this atmosphere of information overload, developing nations may lack the legal and technical resources to draft their own legislation. They often resort to copying the laws of more developed nations.

The future global unification of patent offices will require public administrators to integrate systems from many nations and standardize application processes. The future of patent offices will show a merger of the administrative systems, not just cooperation between offices. This will look like centralized application systems and globally-standardized forms. This future will require nations with technologically and organizationally more efficient systems to help other nations improve and integrate their patent operations into the new global system.

As the patent offices of developing nations around the world bring their administrative systems up to the same level of technology and efficiency as developed nations and the Trilateral patent offices, they will need the support of developed nations. The European Patent Office (EPO) provides one example of how to accomplish this. Their International Academy, begun in 1977, "offers technical, administrative, and legal training to government officials, patent examiners, prosecutors, patent judges, and patent attorneys for member and future member states" (Sum, 2003, p. 379). Programs like this, focused on training and educating, will provide a critical piece of the puzzle that global standardization of intellectual property control has become.

Upgrading and interfacing technology systems presents challenges, but it also presents an opportunity. As these patent offices develop and grow, public health agencies have a chance to network and connect with them, and to make sure that public health concerns are given priority over commercial interests in their review process. Public health agencies must realize the time to address public health concerns is not after the fact of the patents, but before. Patent offices and public health agencies must reach across the administrative boundaries between their operations to form a unified front against exploitation of their nations by the multinational pharmaceutical companies. In the face of the ongoing HIV/AIDS crisis and the threat of uncontrolled viral outbreaks, the very future of public health depends on their ability to work together, not against each other.

References

Bhattacharya, R. (2008). "Are developing countries going too far on TRIPS? A closer look at the new laws in India." *American Journal of Law & Medicine, 34*(2/3), 395-421.

Correa, C. M. (2001, January). "The TRIPS agreement: How much room for maneuver?" *Journal of Human Development, 2*(1), 79-107. doi:10.1080/14649880120050192

Drahos, P. (2008). "Trust me: Patent offices in developing countries." *American Journal of Law & Medicine, 34*(2/3), 151-174.

Dutfield, G. (2008). "Delivering drugs to the poor: Will the TRIPS amendment help?" *American Journal of Law & Medicine, 34*(2/3), 107-124.

Goodwin, P. E. (2008). "Right idea, wrong result—Canada's Access to Medicines Regime." *American Journal of Law & Medicine, 34*(4), 567-584.

Halbert, D. (2005). "Globalized resistance to intellectual property." *Globalization.* http://globalization.icaap.org/content/v5.2/halbert.html

Häyrinen-Alestalo, M. (2001, July). "Is knowledge-based society a relevant strategy for civil society?" *Current Sociology, 49*(4), 203-218. doi:10.1177/0011392101049004011

Hilton, J. (2005). "In praise of sharing." *EDUCAUSE Review, 40*(3), 72-73.

Kobori, S. (2002, May). "TRIPS and the primacy of public health." *Asia-Pacific Review, 9*(1), 10-19. doi:10.1080/13439000220141550

Lanning, S. (2012). *Concise guide to information literacy*. Santa Barbara, CA: ABC-CLIO, LLC.

Lawson, C. and Pickering, C. (2004, December). "TRIPs-Plus patent privileges—An intellectual property 'cargo cult' in Australia." *Prometheus, 22*(4), 355-377. doi:10.1080/0810902041233131163 2

Leal, R. (2014, Spring). "The next step in gene patents: Association for Molecular Pathology v. Myriad Genetics." *Journal of Art, Technology & Intellectual Property Law, 24*(2), 403-423.

Lopert, R., Gleeson, D. (2013, Spring). "The high price of 'free' trade: U.S. trade agreements and access to medicines." *Journal of Law, Medicine & Ethics, 41*(1), 199-223. doi:10.1111/jlme.12014

May, C. (2006, March). "Escaping the TRIPs' trap: The political economy of free and open source software in Africa." *Political Studies, 54*(1), 123-146. doi:10.1111/j.1467-9248.2006.00569.x

Outterson, K. (2008). "Should access to medicines and TRIPS flexibilities be limited to specific diseases?" *American Journal of Law & Medicine, 34*(2/3), 279-301.

Shah, A. K., Warsh, J., Kesselheim, A. (2013, Winter). "The ethics of intellectual property rights in an era of globalization." *Journal of Law, Medicine & Ethics, 41*(4), 841-851. doi:10.1111/jlme.12094

Sum, N. (2003, September). "Informational capitalism and U.S. economic hegemony: Resistance and adaptations in East Asia." *Critical Asian Studies, 35*(3), 373-398.

Van Puymbroeck, R. V. (2010, Fall). "Basic survival needs and access to medicines—Coming to grips with TRIPS: conversion

+ calculation." *Journal of Law, Medicine & Ethics, 38*(3), 520-549. doi:10.1111/j.1748-720X.2010.00510.x

Walker, S. (2001). "The implications of TRIPS: Ethics, health, and human rights." *Journal of Human Development, 2*(1), 109-114. doi:10.1080/14649880120050200

(WHO) World Health Organization (2013, April). *WHO model list of essential medicines, 18th ed.* Retrieved November 20, 2014 from http://apps.who.int/iris/bitstream/10665/93142/1/EML_18_eng .pdf

(WIPO) World Intellectual Property Organization. "What is intellectual property?" http://www.wipo.int/about-ip/en/

9

Leading the Pack:
Australia's Plain Packaging Laws and Tobacco Control Measures Define the Growing International Conflict between Public Health Policy and Intellectual Property Rights

I. Introduction.

The global response to Australia's tobacco control measures reveals the complexity of international politics where trade agreements about intellectual property come into conflict with public health policy. The Australian measures taken to fulfill its commitment as a signatory party to the World Health Organization's Framework Convention on Tobacco Control gave tobacco companies occasion to sue the federal government for infringement on their brands. As more and more FCTC signatory countries begin to adopt measures like Australia's, tobacco companies and nations where they have major operations have brought disputes to the World Trade Organization. Certain trade restrictions brought about in the name of public health, they claim, violate various articles of TRIPS, the international agreement on Trade Related aspects of Intellectual Property Rights. The outcome of these disputes remains to be seen, with the World Trade Organization expecting to issue a decision on a major dispute in 2016. However, Australia's highest federal courts have supported these measures and denied claims to tobacco companies. It comes as little surprise, since these measures originated from advocates at the federal level from nations federally committed to the Framework Convention on Tobacco Control. Will the World Trade Organization similarly uphold tobacco control policies at the international level?

This essay will review the political and judicial history of the Australian tobacco control measures, specifically with regards to "plain packaging" laws but including related measures of their comprehensive policies. This paper will highlight the strong support for the effectiveness of Australia's measures by the national and international research teams publishing analytical evaluations of them. The effects these measures have had on other nations include a wave of trade agreement disputes, but the United Kingdom's recent adoption of similar plain packaging laws scheduled to take effect in 2016 suggests a confidence the World Trade Organization will not be an unconquerable obstacle to the wave of nations fulfilling their commitments to the

Framework Convention on Tobacco Control and radically changing the face of tobacco sales around the world.

II. Origins of Australia's Plain Packaging Laws.

Three years ago, the BBC News reported on "new" restrictions on cigarette packaging in Australia. Packs of cigarettes, they revealed, would come in a drab, dark brown color without any tobacco company logos or colors. The Australian federal government set this public health policy as part of a larger effort to reduce the number of smokers in their country to less than 10 percent by 2018 (Kennedy, 2012). But the story of the graphic health warnings and drab brown packaging now sold in Australia at a heavily taxed price go back to 2003, when the World Health Organization's Framework Convention on Tobacco Control opened for ratification by nations who become signatories to it. The USA signed the WHO's Framework Convention on Tobacco Control in 2004 (UN, 2015). Joining USA and Australia were 166 other nations who signed the Framework Convention on Tobacco Control between its opening in May 2003 and its closing on June 29, 2004, though its ratification by additional nations since then brings the total to 180 (WHO FCTC, 2015). Nations can still join today, through a one-step process of ratification.

The recent Australian policies continue a trend of increasing federal restrictions on tobacco advertising in Australia. Australia began with a ban on TV and radio tobacco ads in 1976, continuing with a ban on tobacco sponsorship of sporting events in 1992 (Kennedy, 2012). But with the advent of the Framework Convention on Tobacco Control, even more push for tobacco control has come from the Australian federal government.

In 2011, the Cancer Council of Australia provided research which "suggested that packaging plays an important part in encouraging young people to try cigarettes" (Kennedy, 2012). The Australian government calculated 15,000 Australian smokers died annually at a cost of AU$30 billion (ibid, 2012). Bolstered by these reports, Attorney-General Nicola Roxon introduced plain packaging legislation during her service as Health Minister, backed by strong advocacy from health groups like the Australian Medical Association (Hambleton, 2012, p. 199). The plain packaging policies, with such strong federal support, became law in 2011 and began sweeping the states in 2012. But soon enough, resistance from multinational tobacco companies began at the national level, spreading quickly into litigation and arbitration affecting many nations around the world.

III. Resistance to Australia's Plain Packaging Laws.

National Resistance. British American Tobacco Australia, Japan Tobacco International, Philip Morris, and Imperial Tobacco Australia challenged the plain packaging policy in the Australian High Court (ibid, p.199). These companies argued "the new measures amounted to the acquisition of their brands by the Government without just compensation, and should be ruled unconstitutional." But, while the High Court admitted the policy "regulated the plaintiffs' intellectual property rights and imposed controls," the Commonwealth of Australia gained no "proprietary benefit or interest" from them (ibid, p. 199). The court ruled the new laws constitutional.

The *American Journal of Law & Medicine* explained the judicial response to the tobacco company claims of trademark infringement. It is worth considering the legal reasoning in the High Court's ruling on the constitutionality of the plain packaging laws, because Philip Morris International will be objecting to the World Trade Organization with similar intellectual property arguments. The High Court heard arguments which hinged on the "bedrock principle" which defines acquisition, and reviewed whether or not the Commonwealth of Australia had acquired (as legally defined) anything in the process of regulating cigarette packaging. Australian law holds that no acquisition of property takes place without the acquiring party gaining an interest in the property, "however slight or insubstantial" that interest may be (Liberman, 2013, p. 370). The resulting legal arguments focused on whether or not the Commonwealth had acquired any interest in the intellectual property (trademarks) and the property (the packages) of the tobacco companies in the new packaging. Tobacco lawyers claimed many interests gained by the Commonwealth, such as free advertising for Quitline now that the smoking cessation hotline's number must appear on all cigarette packs (ibid, p. 371). The High Court did not acknowledge any of the interest claims and granted the tobacco companies nothing.

In fact, the High Court used none of the many arguments it had proposed in a preliminary document, arguments in favor of the public health benefits of plain packaging, the government's power to restrict intellectual property rights in the service of the greater public good, and the obligations Australia has now as part of the Framework Convention on Tobacco Control (ibid, p. 377-9). Instead, The High Court ruled the government had gained no interest in the intellectual property, specifically the brands and trademarks of the tobacco companies, and therefore could regulate their packaging as they liked. Case closed.

The simplicity of the High Court's rejection of the claims may or may not foreshadow impending decisions from the World Trade Organization. But they do shine a spotlight on the battle for supremacy between public health and intellectual property rights in courts. Much like the Australian Federal Court's recent ruling on patenting human DNA sequences in *Myriad Genetics*, decisions may hinge on interpreting the legal definition of a phrase or even a single word. In *Myriad*, the phrases were "artificially created state of affairs" and "matter of manufacture" (D'arcy, 2014). Here, the word in question was acquisition. One might expect that, as the court did in their preliminary documents, cases affecting public health will depend on evaluating the benefits they provide to people. But in reality, the argument over the definition of a single word can mark the turning point in who wins: public health policy as envisioned by the World Health Organization or the corporate intellectual property rights enshrined in the World Trade Organization.

International Resistance. In today's globalized political environment, the legal questions do not end at the federal level. Australia's ruling has resulted in litigation at the international level. Tobacco-exporting nations the Dominican Republic, Ukraine, and Honduras have challenged the plain packaging laws through disputes registered with the World Trade Organization (Hambleton, 2012, p. 199). Ukraine's involvement in the dispute may seem odd, because it does not currently export tobacco into Australia (Morran, 2015). Why does Ukraine suddenly care about the Australian market?

Philip Morris International, one of the defeated plaintiffs in the Australian High Court, has had operations in Ukraine since 1994 when it "acquired a majority share of the JSC Kharkiv tobacco factory. In 1996 the factory started manufacturing the first international PMI brands in Ukraine: *Chesterfield* and *Bond Street*. In 2000, the factory began producing *Marlboro*" (PMI, 2015). Philip Morris International created the Philip Morris Ukraine entity which in March 2013 joined the US-Ukraine Business Council (USUBC), a group of "over 200 companies and organizations" with business and investment interest in Ukraine, including "five other Fortune 500 type companies: Amway, DuPont, Ecolab, Intel, and Visa" (USUBC, 2013). With fourteen regional offices and 1400 employees, Philip Morris Ukraine has a significant interest in keeping Ukrainian tobacco exports financially viable.

Begun in 2012, the Ukrainian dispute, numbered by the World Trade Organization as Dispute DS434, has not reached a conclusion. A panel requested by Ukraine formed in May 2014. In October 2014, the panel announced it would issue a final report "not before the first half of 2016" (WTO, 2014). Ukraine's dispute pits Australia's Tobacco Plain Packaging Act against specific articles of the TRIPS agreement and two other trade agreements: first, GATT, the General Agreement on Tariffs and Trade, with its original 1947 provisions still in effect as modified under the World Trade Organization which replaced it in 1994; and second, the international treaty called the Agreement on Technical Barriers to Trade (or more simply, TBT Agreement) which also coincides with the 1994 creation of the World Trade Organization and became effective in 1995 (WTO, 2014).

Philip Morris has even more fronts where it fights its private war for rights to sell an addictive and dangerous product. Reports in the press accuse Philip Morris International of "shifting control of its Australian cigarette operations to Hong Kong-based Philip Morris Asia" for the express purpose of, less than a year later, suing "the Australian government through an international court, saying the government's plan to force all cigarettes into plain non-branded packaging violated a decades-old trade agreement with Hong Kong" (Morran, 2015). In response, Philip Morris International openly confirms their position that "Australia's plain packaging policy is an unprecedented destruction of brands and breaches Australia's treaty with Hong Kong" (PMI, 2014). The Hong Kong question is one of two Investor State Dispute Settlements now in arbitration and publicly defended in statements by Philip Morris International. The other involves Uruguay.

Uruguay joined the numerous national parties now requesting a consultation on Australia's laws from the World Trade Organization in DS434 (WTO, 2014). But Uruguay's problems with Philip Morris pre-date Australia's plain packaging laws. Philip Morris International dragged Uruguay into arbitration in 2010, claiming that Investor State Dispute Settlement (ISDS) provisions of international trade agreements protected their intellectual property in the forms of branded packaging with trademarks (PMI, 2014). Philip Morris International's public statement on its ISDS cases against Australia (via Hong Kong) and Uruguay are "about governments destroying our... intellectual property. In doing so, both governments violated their pledge under binding international treaties not to deprive investors of their property without fair compensation in return" (PMI, 2014).

Uruguay developed its own policy about graphic warnings on cigarette packages, mandating coverage of 80 percent of the entire package with these warnings. But in addition to this policy which is even more aggressive than Australia's, Uruguay introduced a "ban on selling more than one variant of each cigarette brand," thus preventing Philip Morris from offering a wide range of their brands. And this measure, claims Philip Morris, "violates Uruguay's treaty with Switzerland" (PMI, 2014).

In Uruguay, the potential legal victory for Philip Morris would not be changing the laws. It would be a cash payoff. The treaty with Switzerland is the Uruguay-Switzerland Bilateral Investment Treaty (BIT). Philip Morris International claims Uruguay's laws "caused a substantial decrease in sales and a deprivation of intellectual property rights" which entitles PMI to compensation under the treaty (Sahin, 2014). If Australia's High Court has dashed Philip Morris International's hopes of regaining branded packaging, the company remains steadfastly determined to bilk entire nations for payments to compensate for its reduced sales. After their utterly unconvincing arguments about intellectual property infringements in the Australian High Court, the Philip Morris legal team may have nothing left to do but salvage as much cash money as possible on the way down.

It may not be entirely wasted effort. Philip Morris International and its subsidiaries have products for sale in 180 countries, a number now exactly equal to the number of nations ratifying the WHO Framework Convention on Tobacco Control (USUBC, 2013). Philip Morris International could easily spend decades as a parasite on the public funds and resources of nation after nation. Philip Morris could easily pay its lawyers to keep wasting the time and resources of international organizations while attempting to keep its cash flow positive and its markets as open to exploitation as possible.

IV. Ethical Considerations of Plain Packaging Laws.

Government Investment in Tobacco Companies. Aside from the litigation and trade disputes from tobacco-producing companies and tobacco-exporting nations, no one in the public voices any strong ethical objections to these laws. Neither academic journals nor the current-events media have tales of citizen groups seeking to reclaim their freedom to enjoy colorful tobacco packaging with interactive advertising promotions and distinctive brands. The only ethical questions from scholars and health advocates involve the consistency of these measures with other government activities.

For example, the Australian government has a "$73 billion Future Fund set up to offset future public servant superannuation liabilities" (Hambleton, 2012, p. 200). These liabilities are merely a type of tax payment made by Australian companies based on their employee's earnings, per the Australian Taxation Office (ATO, 2015). The government makes investments to cover its future tax payments on its employees. What do they invest in? Recently, the fund invested "almost $38 million... in tobacco company shares between December 2010, and February, 2012" (Hambleton, 2012, p.200). Clearly, different offices of the same federal government can pursue conflicting policy goals. It would not be surprising to see future guidelines developed by the Conference of Parties to the Framework Convention on Tobacco Control to ensure governments are not investing in the same companies parasitizing them for cash payments through lengthy and costly litigation.

More Regulation, Not Less. Tobacco's well-documented links to disease and death, facts the tobacco industry no longer bothers to deny, make it a cause to which not even avid smokers can enthusiastically rally. Few come out in support of "the multinational cigarette companies that have created a virtual money-printing machine" by using "trademarks to compete on image rather than price." True, "governments, the broader business community, and members of the public" do have concerns about losing the tobacco industry as a source of revenue (Sweanor, 2011, p. 683). From the Australian government's Future Fund to the owners and franchisees of small retail shops, to the peddlers of black market chop-chop, tobacco is a proven source of revenue. But the public wants still more restriction on tobacco, not less.

In the United States, anti-smoking groups such as Action on Smoking & Health have criticized their federal government's level of response to its commitment to the Framework Convention on Tobacco Control, accusing it of "sitting on the sidelines of this historic and vital effort" (ASH, 2012). While the USA has not taken such drastic control of packaging at the federal level, it has made other recent restrictions that are in compliance with the established guidelines of the FCTC, and it has done so despite powerful political lobbies from major tobacco companies with historical power bases in the states. For example, what happened to Camel Lights? Now, they are Camel Blue. Marlboro Lights? Now Marlboro Gold. This shift complies with a Framework Convention on Tobacco Control guideline about not allowing packaging that promotes lighter cigarettes as a potentially healthier or less dangerous option than a "full-flavored" cigarette.

But for the most part, the U.S. federal government seems content to let states take the initiative. Arizona and other states have begun to follow California's lead in banning smoking in public places, with many cities like Boston working to ban even eCigs which contain no tobacco and do not create smoke. It would not be surprising to see American state initiatives similar to Framework Convention on Tobacco Control commitments evolving at their own pace just as Australia's different states adopted their smoking cessation signs at their own pace, and with different severity levels to the warnings.

V. Evaluating Australia's Tobacco Control Measures.

Conference of Parties. Nations who have ratified the Framework Convention on Tobacco Control make up the Conference of Parties. Members of this group evaluate and establish guidelines for tobacco control, including "a set of policy options and recommendations on economically sustainable alternatives to tobacco growing" (WHO FCTC, 2015). To date, the conference has determined eight solid guidelines they believe will further the FCTC's goals, with the full text of each guideline published at http://www.who.int/fctc/guidelines/adopted/en/. Generally, the eight guidelines are:

- Protection of public health policies with respect to tobacco control from commercial and other vested interests of the tobacco industry.
- Price and tax measures to reduce the demand for tobacco.
- Protection from exposure to tobacco smoke.
- Regulation of the contents of tobacco products and regulation of tobacco product disclosures.
- Packaging and labelling of tobacco products.
- Education, communication, training, and public awareness.
- Tobacco advertising, promotion, and sponsorship.
- Demand reduction measures concerning tobacco dependence and cessation.

The Conference of Parties has addressed questions about tobacco as a revenue source from the agricultural and production perspective in addition to the retail and point of sale perspective. Their recent report *Policy Options and Recommendations on Economically Sustainable Alternatives to Tobacco Growing* attempts to answer the question, "What will farmers grow when tobacco control measures reduce global tobacco demand?" In fact, the report says that time is now, and it calls the need to find income alternatives for farming and processing facilities "urgent" (WHO, 2015).

The Conference of Parties is far, far ahead of the pack in evaluating the global effects of Framework Convention on Tobacco Control measures and plain packaging. The Conference of Parties concludes the efforts are demonstrably working. The Conference of Parties is already collaborating on a solid, workable set of guidelines to minimize economic disruption, reclaim the environment from the harmful effects of tobacco farming, and protect sustainable alternatives from being bullied by the interests of tobacco companies. These are outlined in the principles of the report. The report also recommends educational and training programs to be developed after study of community groups by gender, age, education, and ethnicity to help target the programs to them. At the level of the World Health

Organization, the contentious twentieth-century debates about potential harm to health and environment from the tobacco industry have been settled long ago. Their only question is, "What next?"

Joint Efforts at the National Level. This forward-thinking attitude of the Conference of Parties is consistent with other published research on plain packaging laws and related tobacco control measures. Evaluations of the plain packaging laws took place before they even began, as research groups sought to predict whether or not they would work in practice. A UK-based research team funded by the Department of Health presented a predictive analysis of whether or not plain packaging would meet the "the guidelines for the International Framework Convention on Tobacco Control: reduced appeal, increased salience and effectiveness of health warnings, and more accurate perceptions of product strength and harm" (Stead, 2013, p.1). By using the FCTC guidelines, the research team reveals the international community's interest in seeing how well Australia's efforts play out on the global stage. This team predicted that plain, dark, standardized packaging would meet all of the FCTC guidelines.

At the national level, the academic community and public health agencies collaborate to evaluate other aspects of tobacco control. For example, research into controlling black market tobacco brought the School of Economics, Finance, and Marketing from RMIT University in Melbourne together with the Center for Population Health, MacFarlane Burnet Institute for Medical Research and Public Health. Working together, these two groups provided empirical evidence about smokers' decisions to smoke chop-chop, a black market form of tobacco which has often been cured and processed outside of the regulatory oversight mandated for legal tobacco production for health reasons. Policy about black market tobacco plays a small but noteworthy role in supporting the broad goal of the plain packaging policy: reducing smoking to less than 10 percent nationally.

The team challenged the prevailing belief that smokers choose chop-chop based on its lower price. The researchers concluded lower price is not the dominant factor in choosing chop-chop over legal tobacco. Instead, their survey suggests availability of black market tobacco was the primary factor in choosing it over legal tobacco. Most former chop-chop smokers now smoking legal tobacco cited lack of availability as their primary motivation for the switch. The researchers concluded with a prediction: Policies aimed at curbing illegal tobacco use through price controls will not be successful, but policies which can reduce the illegal supply will be (Pellegrini, 2011, p. 387).

International Tobacco Control Policy Evaluation Project. National public health departments and university researchers are not the only ones examining Australia from an international guidelines perspective. The International Tobacco Control Policy Evaluation Project exists precisely to study measures like the ones in Australia. Its International Tobacco Control Four Country Survey, or ITC-4, examined one of the supporting measures of Australia's comprehensive polices: point of sale signage warning about tobacco's health risks and posting a smoking cessation hotline in big, bold text. The research team behind the ITC-4 compared mandates about the size, color, text, content, and placement of these signs within various Australian states. The team concluded the anti-smoking signs at retail outlets in Australia correlated to a significant, upward, linear trend in awareness of the signs. The team further correlated this increased awareness with increased interest in quitting smoking, and with increased attempts to do so (Li, 2012, p. 429).

The authors of the study proposed the effectiveness of the signs depends on more than their large size, clear text, simple message, and unmistakable presence in shops. The signs work in tandem with a whole set of policies in different media, and the point of sale warnings are reinforced by the packaging warnings (ibid, p. 430). The researchers also pointed out that individual Australian states had their own timetables for rolling out the signs, with their policies going into effect at different times and with the requirements for the signs varying in intensity from state to state, though strengthened by the less severe states over time (ibid, p. 428).

Though it is too early to have a vast body of published peer-reviewed research on all the long-term effects of plain packaging laws, a wide body of research supports the policies at the academic level, the federal level, and the international level. Australia may soon have data showing whether or not they have reached their stated policy goal of fewer than 10 percent of the population smoking. The most recent statistics on tobacco use from the Australian Department of Health were released in 2014, covering 2013 data. The trend of smoking reduction continues year over year in Australia, down now to 12.8 percent of the population aged 14 or over being daily smokers, and 13.3 percent of people aged 18 or over. These numbers are roughly half the figures from ten years prior (25 percent and 26.1 percent, respectively) (DOH, 2015). Australia's comprehensive efforts and unified federal front have nearly succeeded. Perhaps 2015's data published in 2016 will show they already have.

VI. Conclusion.

Australia has paved the way by acting as a case study for other Framework Convention on Tobacco Control signatory nations. The United Kingdom voted on March 16, 2015 to adopt plain packaging laws similar to Australia's and plans to introduce plain packaging in May, 2016 (WHO FCTC, 2015). Ireland voted to implement plain packaging laws early in March, followed shortly by England, with more United Kingdom members announcing they will, too. The widespread majority support for these measures is apparent from the overwhelming parliamentary approval in England where "The House of Commons voted 367 to 113 in favour of packaging which is uniform in shape, size and design, featuring only the brand name and the usual graphic health warnings. The bill passed through the House of Lords without a vote" (Richardson, 2015).

As one public health advocate noted at the inception of Australia's plain packaging policy, "Contextual factors and the lack of opportunity to undertake controlled experiments mean that one can never predict with certainty what the effect will be"

(West 2011, p. 681). But now, four years later, the international community has a good idea of the litigation that will follow in federal and international courts. Nations now have an example of the way such litigation will hinge on questions of intellectual property rights defined by international trade agreements. Nations might expect tobacco companies to spend resources pursuing compensation instead of offering outright resistance to infringement as country after country adopts similar measures.

Plain packaging has gained nearly unilateral support from the academic and research communities, public health agencies, politicians and federal officials, advocacy groups, the medical community, the 180 signatory nations to the Framework Convention on Tobacco Control, and the highest courts in the land. The only serious objectors to plain packaging and other FCTC-based measures to control tobacco remain the companies which profit from tobacco sales, and nations exporting it for sale, especially those where said companies have significant overseas operations despite their origins as U.S.-based corporations. Australia has successfully implemented these policies on a widespread basis with cooperation from its states. Australia has successfully prevented, so far, its public funds from being parasitized by compensatory payments to multinational tobacco companies.

All of this bodes well for other nations seeking similar policy measures to achieve a statistical reduction in tobacco use, leaving the tobacco companies with little recourse but to go to the World Trade Organization. By the end of 2016, the signatory nations of the Framework Convention on Tobacco Control will know whether or not the WTO will favor public health over intellectual property rights, and just what form that legal reasoning will take. The World Trade Organization's position on tobacco control through packaging restrictions on brand and trademark usage will set yet another precedent in the ongoing political power struggle between corporate profit interests and people's health on an international level.

References

Action on Smoking & Health (ASH). (August 7, 2012). "ASH calls on President Obama to immediately submit FCTC for ratification, 8 years after U.S. signed agreement." https://ash.org/ash-calls-on-public-to-urge-obama-senate-to-ratify-whos-framework-convention-on-tobacco-control/#sthash.jHPoeTat.dpuf

Australian Government, Department of Health. (May 6, 2015). "Tobacco key facts and figures: National Drug Strategy Household Survey detailed report 2013." http://www.health.gov.au/internet/main/publishing.nsf/Content/tobacco-kff

Australian Tax Office. (2015). "Superannuation payments." https://www.ato.gov.au/Business/Employers/Payments-and-reporting/Superannuation-payments/

D'Arcy v. Myriad Genetics Inc [2014] FCAFC 115 (2014, September 5). *Federal Court of Australia.* http://www.austlii.edu.au/au/cases/cth/FCAFC/2014/115.html

Hambleton, Steve. (November, 2012). "World-leading plain packaging laws squeeze big tobacco." *World Medical Journal,* 58(5/6): 199-200.

Kennedy, Duncan. (Dec. 1, 2012). "Australian smokers given plain packs." *BBC News Sydney.* http://www.bbc.com/news/world-asia-20559585

Li, Lin, et. al. (Feb. 2012). "The association between exposure to point-of-sale anti-smoking warnings and smokers' interest in quitting and quit attempts: findings from the International Tobacco Control Four Country Survey." *Addiction, 107*(2): 425-433. DOI: 10.1111/j.1360-0443.2011.03668.x

Liberman, Jonathan. (2013). "Plainly constitutional: the upholding of plain tobacco packaging by the high court of Australia." *American Journal of Law & Medicine*, 39(2/3): 361-381.

Morran, Chris. (February 16, 2015). "Meet the new Marlboro spokesman: Jeff, the diseased lung in a cowboy hat." *Consumerist.* http://consumerist.com/2015/02/16/meet-the-new-marlboro-spokesman-jeff-the-diseased-lung-in-a-cowboy-hat/

Pellegrini, Breanna, et. al. (Oct. 2011). "Understanding the motivations of contraband tobacco smokers." *Drugs: Education, Prevention & Policy*, 18(5): 387-392. DOI: 10.3109/09687637.2011.562935. http://www.researchgate.net/profile/Breanna_Pellegrini/publication/232057905_Understanding_the_motivations_of_contraband_tobacco_smokers/links/0c960519d87d815102000000.pdf

Philip Morris International (PMI). (October 13, 2014). "Trade agreements and ISDS: protecting public interest and investors." http://justthefacts.pmi.com/international-trade-agreements-and-isds-protecting-the-intellectual-property-rights-of-legal-business/

Philip Morris International (PMI). (2015). "Country overview: Ukraine." http://www.pmi.com/marketpages/Pages/market_en_ua.aspx#

Richardson, Hayley. (March 16, 2015). "UK passes law to require plain cigarette packaging in England." *Newsweek.* http://europe.newsweek.com/uk-passes-law-require-plain-cigarette-packaging-england-314110

Sahin, Aylin A. (November 7, 2014). "Philip Morris vs. Uruguay: intellectual property debate in international investment arbitration." *Berkeley Technology Law Journal.* http://btlj.org/2014/11/philip-morris-vs-uruguay-intellectual-property-debate-in-international-investment-arbitration/

Stead, Martine et. al. (October, 2013). "Is consumer response to plain/standardised tobacco packaging consistent with Framework Convention on Tobacco Control guidelines? A Systematic Review of Quantitative Studies." *PLoS ONE, 8*(10): 1-10. DOI: 10.1371/journal.pone.0075919

Sweanor, David T. (Nov. 2011). "Effective beats dramatic: A commentary on Australia's plain packaging of cigarettes." *Drug & Alcohol Review, 30*(6): 683-684. DOI: 10.1111/j.1465-3362.2011.00370.x

United Nations (UN). (2015) Status as at 10-05-2015 06:48:08 EDT. *United Nation Treaty Collection.* https://treaties.un.org/pages/ViewDetails.aspx?src=TREATY&mtdsg_no=IX-4&chapter=9&lang=en

US-Ukraine Business Council (USUBC). (March 11, 2013). "Philip Morris Ukraine joins U.S.-Ukraine Business Council (USUBC)." http://www.usubc.org/site/member-news/philip-morris-ukraine-joins-u-s-ukraine-business-council-usubc

West, Robert. (Nov. 2011). "Preventing tobacco companies from advertising using their packaging could be an important component of comprehensive tobacco control: A commentary on Australia's plain packaging of cigarettes." *Drug & Alcohol Review, 30*(6): 681-682. DOI: 10.1111/j.1465-3362.2011.00369.x

World Health Organization (WHO). (2015). "Guidelines and policy options and recommendations for implementation of the WHO FCTC." http://www.who.int/fctc/guidelines/adopted/en/

World Health Organization (WHO). (2015) "Policy options and recommendations on economically sustainable alternatives to tobacco growing (in relation to articles 17 and 18 of the WHO FCTC)."
http://www.who.int/fctc/guidelines/adopted/Policy_options_reccommendations_Articles17_18_COP6.pdf

WHO Framework on Tobacco Control (WHO FCTC). (2015). "Global domino effect in implementing plain packaging." (Announcement on UK vote on plain packaging).
http://www.who.int/fctc/en/

World Trade Organization (WTO). (October 30, 2014). "Dispute Settlement: Dispute DS434: Australia: certain measures concerning trademarks and other plain packaging requirements applicable to tobacco products and packaging."
https://www.wto.org/english/tratop_e/dispu_e/cases_e/ds434_e.htm

10

Policy Alternatives to Water Fluoridation

I. Introduction.
II. Who Decides to Fluoridate a City's Water?
    The Federal Government's Role.
    Decisions at the Municipal Level.
III. The Chemicals Used in Fluoridation.
    Sodium Fluoride.
    Sodium Fluorosilicate.
    Hydrofluorosilicic Acid.
IV. What Does it Cost to Fluoridate?
    Example Fluoridation Costs for Three Cities.
    Indirect Cost Reduction to Citizens.
V. What are the Dental Health Benefits of Fluoride?
    Fluoride versus the Real Cause of Tooth Decay.
    Dental Health Benefits of Topical Fluoride Use.
VI. What are the Health Risks of Ingesting Fluoride?
    Fluoride and Prozac.
    Fluoride and the Thyroid.
    Dosage.
VII. Policy Options for Citizens.
    Elements of a Comprehensive Alternative.
    Options for Those Who Cannot Stop Fluoridation.
VIII. Conclusion.

References

I. Introduction.

In recent interviews, former Minnesota governor Jesse Ventura has advocated an end to adding fluoride to municipal water supplies. He has claimed the Nazis used fluoride in drinking water to pacify people (Isquith, 2014). Ventura has claimed that fluoride is an ingredient in Prozac, and the USA has been effectively dosing its citizens with mood-altering chemicals. Is there any truth to Ventura's confrontational statements about fluoridation? Jay Lehr, author of *The Fluoride Wars*, told interviewers from a Florida newspaper, "The World War II death camp statement is an absurd lie" (Bowers, 2011). But one can easily look up the chemical composition of Prozac and verify it contains fluorine atoms.

For every refuted claim about fluoridation, a new one seems to appear. Paul Connett, PhD, executive director of the Fluoride Action Network, published fifty reasons to oppose in fluoridation in 2004. He continues to present his arguments to municipalities like Dallas, TX, where the January 2015 renewal of a fluoridation contract recently reopened the fluoride debate (Activists, 2014). Connett's reasons range from the cumulative effects of fluoride as a poison, to questioning some studies which link fluoride to decreased rates of tooth decay (Connett, 2004, p. 70-74).

In this atmosphere of conflicting claims and seemingly contradictory information, fluoridation remains a contentious public health policy in the twenty-first century. Both peer-reviewed research and celebrity claims ride a rising tide of public inquiry into the long-accepted practice of fluoridation. The first controlled municipal water fluoridation trial began in 1945 in the USA (Lennon, 2006, p. 759). But 70 years later, citizens continue to argue its merits in city councils and on public ballots across the country. This paper will look at some of those cities.

This paper will also establish, in plain language, facts agreed upon by both sides of the debate, and propose alternative policy measures which simultaneously meet the needs of fluoride supporters and objectors alike. It will give examples of current fluoridation policies in well-known cities, review the claims about health risks and benefits, and provide a clear explanation of what fluoridation really means in chemical terms. The political realities of changing a fluoride policy require not just cooperation between city councils and their constituents, but between two groups with apparently conflicting public health concerns: one concerned about tooth decay, and one concerned about drinking a toxic chemical. That both of these groups seek to advance the cause of public health provides an opportunity for them to collaborate and bring mutually agreeable, politically feasible policies to a public referendum.

II. Who Decides to Fluoridate a City's Water?

If citizens feel concerned the government is fluoridating their water, they first need clarity about which government is involved. The federal government does have a role in setting limits of fluoride in water systems, but the decision to fluoridate comes from municipal governments in most states, and from the state government in a minority of states.

The Federal Government's Role. The federal government does not set fluoridation policy, though federal agencies offer recommendations, and the Environmental Protection Agency (EPA) mandates an upper limit to fluoride content. In April 2015, the US Department of Health & Human Services (HHS) issued a new recommendation for the optimum level of fluoridation, now set at 0.7 milligrams per liter of water. This represents the lower limit of their previous range of 0.7–1.2 mg/L, a range unchanged since HHS issued it in 1962 (HHS, 2015).

This new recommendation is not a mandate to states and municipalities. However, in cities like Boulder, CO, a resulting review of current policy is already underway, including obtaining non-binding recommendations from state governmental agencies like the Colorado Department of Public Health and Environment (Linenfelser, 2015). Boulder's Water Quality Manager explained the review will include an evaluation of whether or not adjusting the fluoridation process to the new target level would still meet the intent of the existing policy.

For some cities, the new federal recommendation has given administrators an opportunity to review policy, but their fluoridation levels are already close to the target. For example, a 1993 census of fluoride levels in Arizona showed Phoenix targeting an optimum level of 0.7 mg/L (HHS, 1993, p. 47). The city's annual water analysis for 2014 shows a minimum fluoride level of 0.5 mg/L and a maximum level of 0.8 mg/L, with average levels at 0.6 mg/L (City of Phoenix, 2014, p.2). This annual analysis by the Water Services Department tests levels at approximately twenty-two different sites (Espericueta, 2015). Phoenix is already very close to its historical target and the new HHS recommendation.

Federal mandate on fluoride comes from the Environmental Protection Agency. The EPA sets a legal cap on the amount of fluoride in public water systems, a cap called the Maximum Contaminant Level (MCL). This cap is public knowledge and appears on the EPA's website about fluoride in drinking water as 4 mg/L. The EPA also sets a secondary level at 2 mg/L, a level intended to prevent a well-documented discoloration in children's teeth which results from excessive fluoride. This secondary level is not mandated, but the EPA does require public water systems to notify them when average levels exceed this threshold (EPA, 2011). *Note:* The measurements of milligrams per liter convert directly to a "parts per million" figure. 4 mg/L equals 4 ppm (EPA, 2015).

Decisions at the Municipal Level. Aside from the federally mandated Maximum Contaminant Level, the decision to fluoridate remains a city or county decision in most states. A minority of states mandate fluoridation for the entire state, and the laws vary somewhat in establishing the minimum size of communities covered by the mandate, and also in their requirements for a public referendum to approve fluoridation (Juneau, 2006, p. 98-101). Therefore, in most U.S. cities, control of fluoridation rests in the hands of voters at the municipal level, and in fewer cases at the state level.

However, it is not always as simple as taking a vote. In Boulder, CO, for example, voters in 2006 had an opportunity to reconsider the fluoridation policy begun in 1969. A ballot initiative gained enough signatures to put fluoride to a public vote. A majority of voters decided to continue fluoridating Boulder's water, though the city's Water Quality Manager reports the measure was only "barely defeated" (Linenfelser, 2015).

A public referendum does not always happen. In 2012, a sub-committee of the city council in Phoenix, AZ addressed concerns about fluoridation. The question of fluoridation was not a ballot initiative in this case, but a matter brought before the city council due to one citizen's concerns about her hypothyroidism (Forsythe, 2012). A council sub-committee heard testimony from chemistry professors, dentists, and public health administrators, but no vote was held. The council sub-committee members agreed to continue the fluoridation policy without taking a vote and without bringing the matter before the full city council for review (Gardiner, 2012). The matter of fluoridation was settled by only a sub-committee of a city council.

Local politics clearly play a role in these decisions. Furthermore, a city council does not always agree with the public when fluoridation is put on the ballot. For example, the city council of Portland, OR voted in 2012 to begin fluoridation, only to have voters refuse fluoridation on the ballot the following May (Innes, 2014).

In some cases, local implementation faces not political challenges but practical ones. In Tucson, AZ, local dentists persuaded their mayor and city council to begin fluoridation in 1992, without resorting to a ballot initiative. But more than two decades later, the fluoridation has not begun. The "first attempt to deliver the water was disastrous, and Tucson Water scrapped a single-point facility, which was part of the original fluoridation plan" (ibid, 2014). A plan to begin fluoridation includes constructing the facility and obtaining equipment to do the job, and this requires planning and budget considerations as well as architectural ones.

Therefore, the decision to fluoridate municipal water systems falls partly to municipal governments, including their administrators, and partly to voters, with voters having recourse to ballot initiatives if they disagree with city council. Regardless of mandate, the logistical and infrastructure realities of a community can determine whether or not the city can truly take action. One would also expect this to hold true even in the minority of states mandating fluoridation from the state level.

III. The Chemicals Used in Fluoridation.

Questions over the toxicity of fluoride must address the specific chemicals used to add it to water systems. The EPA's Maximum Contaminant Level concerns fluoride specifically. But fluoride, a negatively charged ion of the element fluorine, is never added directly to public water systems in the fluoridation process. To fluoridate water, cities choose to use one of three chemicals: sodium fluoride, hydrofluorosilicic acid, and sodium fluorosilicate. (Sodium fluorosilicate, Na_2SiF_6, is also known as sodium silicofluoride or disodium hexafluorosilicate. Hydrofluorosilicic acid, H_2SiF_6, is also called fluorosilicic acid, or HFS, or FSA in the literature.) Each of these three chemicals has a Material Data Safety Sheet, a document well-known to American workers as required for all hazardous substances in workplaces, per the Occupational Safety & Health Administration (OSHA).

Sodium Fluoride. Sodium fluoride is the active ingredient in over-the-counter fluoride mouthwash. The ingredients label on a bottle of ACT Anticavity Fluoride Rinse, for example, shows an active ingredient of 0.05% sodium fluoride (ACT, 2015). Per the instructions on the bottle, anticavity mouth rinses are meant to be held in the mouth for a minute and spit out, never swallowed.

Is sodium fluoride toxic? The Material Data Safety Sheet says yes. The MSDS for sodium fluoride warns of irritant and corrosive effects to eyes and skin, that it "may be toxic to kidneys, lungs, the nervous system, heart, gastrointestinal tract, cardiovascular system, bones, teeth", that "repeated or prolonged exposure" can cause organ damage, and that "severe over-exposure can result in death" (ScienceLab, 2015). The MSDS continues with warnings to not ingest it or breathe its dust in solid form, and specifically says to "prevent entry into sewers." The chemical is slightly explosive in the presence of heat.

Sodium Fluorosilicate. The MSDS for sodium fluorosilicate (sodium silicofluoride) reads similarly to that of sodium fluoride. It notes the irritant and corrosive effects to eyes and skin, warns against breathing the dust, and mentions repeated exposure may cause the chemical to accumulate in the organs, leading to a "general deterioration" in health. The MSDS includes a warning to "prevent entry into sewers," as well as a warning to "never add water to this product" (ScienceLab, 2015). These warnings seem almost intentionally ironic, considering the chemicals are purchased to be added to the water supply system.

Hydrofluorosilicic Acid. Hydrofluorosilicic acid is a byproduct of phosphate production, specifically phosphate-based fertilizer production. The anti-fluoride website FluorideAlert.org claims the acid is a hazardous waste mostly fertilizer production in Florida (Fluoride Action Network, 2015). Finding facts to prove this statement turns out to be surprisingly easy.

For example, the city of Boulder, CO, uses hydrofluorosilicic acid in its fluoridation program (Boulder, 2015). In a phone interview, Boulder's Water Quality Manager pulled a recent invoice from the supplier for this chemical. The acid comes from a chemical company in Florida called Mosaic (Linenfelser, 2015). Mosaic's web page about hydrofluorosilicic acid confirms it is:

"produced during the concentration of **phosphoric acid** in an evaporation process unique to the **phosphate industry**. The vapor stream from the phosphoric acid reaction is scrubbed with water to form [hydrofluorosilicic acid] from the naturally occurring silica and fluorine in the phosphoric acid." (Mosaic, 2015).

The Mosaic chemical company includes Mosaic CropNutrition, a fertilizer company. The link between hazardous waste from fertilizer manufacturers and the chemicals used in fluoridation is not a hoax, a scare tactic, or a conspiracy theory. It is an easily verifiable fact. When this fact was brought up in a phone interview with the Chief Water Quality Inspector of the

City of Phoenix, he simply agreed (Espericueta, 2015). While the general public may find this connection between fertilizer, hazardous waste, and fluoridation startling or even sinister, public administrators involved in fluoridation are well aware of it and make no attempt to deny it. Safe or not, fluoridation is not a cover-up.

The Material Data Safety Sheet provided on Mosaic's page confirms hydrofluorosilicic acid's toxicity. Like the other two chemicals, it is "corrosive to the skin, eyes, and mucous membranes through direct contact, inhalation, or ingestion." The MSDS warns "overexposure may lead to coma or death." It says "prolonged or repeated exposure to fluoride compounds may cause fluorosis," a condition characterized not only by discolored tooth enamel but by hardening or softening of bones, joint pain, and limited range of motion (Mosaic, 2015). And like the other two chemicals, users are explicitly warned to "prevent discharge into waterways and sewers."

Therefore, claims that water fluoridation puts hazardous waste into public water are partially correct. Sodium fluoride would not be considered a waste product, but its toxicity and hazardous nature are plainly stated on the Material Data Safety Sheet. Hydrofluorosilicic acid is indeed a reclaimed waste from the fertilizer industry, with a clearly documented toxicity and hazardous nature. Sodium fluorosilicate is produced by taking that hydrofluorosilicic acid and neutralizing it with sodium carbonate to produce a solid matter, making it merely one more step removed from its origin as hazardous waste (BFS, 2015).

To summarize so far, the EPA has determined any fluoride concentration above 4 mg/L to be unsafe for consumption and illegal. To reach the historical target range of 0.7–1.2 mg/L recommended for dental health by the HHS, cities must add fluoride-containing chemicals, not pure fluoride. These chemicals are known to be toxic and hazardous, and described as such on their OSHA-mandated Material Safety Data Sheets. The decision to add these chemicals is made on the local and municipal level in most states, and occasionally at the state level. Voters have recourse to public ballot initiatives whether they want to begin or end the addition of these chemicals to their water systems.

IV. What Does It Cost to Fluoridate?

Setting aside the one-time costs of installing a new fluoridation system, the ongoing costs depend on several things. A city's population and water usage determine the volume of its water system, which determines the amount of chemicals needed to reach the target level of fluoridation. The natural level of fluoride in local water also affects how much chemical needs to go in the water to reach the HHS target level. The city pays both the cost of the chemicals and the cost of infrastructure (maintenance, labor, testing) to administer them. Public policy debates over fluoridation compare these costs to the reduction in individual costs to treat tooth decay and the related health problems it causes. Federal sources claim the cost of fluoridation on a per-citizen or per-household basis is offset by preventing far greater costs for care.

Example Fluoridation Costs for Three Cities. The city of Boulder, CO shows on its public fluoridation web page an annual cost of $60,000 to buy hydrofluorosilicic acid (Boulder, 2015). Boulder calculates this cost at approximately 85 cents per household annually. A decision to use a different chemical would affect the cost:

> "There are other options and methods that vary in cost due to pureness of grade, availability, and form (powder or liquid). The preliminary cost estimates to purchase the additive for these options vary from about $25,800 annually to over $1.3 million annually. Some options would require additional capital costs to enable city equipment to use the new product and for employees to safely handle the additive" (Boulder, 2015).

Costs for Dallas, TX are somewhat greater. The Dallas City Council recently reviewed a three-year, $1,060,800 contract for fluoridation expiring in January, 2015 (Mercola, 2014). *The Dallas*

Morning News reported in January the city council voted to continue the contract, with two council members opposed. The beneficiary of this contract is Mosaic CropNutrition (Wilonsky, 2015). Mosaic CropNutrition is a company of Mosaic, Boulder's supplier of hydrofluorosilicic acid, and it is a fertilizer company (Mosaic CropNutrition, 2015).

As of 2012, Phoenix, AZ, spends $420,000 per year for its fluoridation chemicals, part of the total annual cost of $582,000 to fluoridate the water system (City of Phoenix, 2012). Phoenix uses hydrofluorosilicic acid, like Boulder and Dallas, but has a contract with Thatcher Company for the product (Espericueta, 2015). Thatcher Group is a chemical manufacturer and distributor in Utah with a public website at Tchem.com. Thatcher is a supplier of fertilizer products, listed on their site, including the phosphoric acid from which hydrofluorosilicic acid comes (Thatcher, 2015.)

Indirect Cost Reduction to Citizens. The justification of these costs is the simultaneous reduction in health care costs for a city's citizens. A pamphlet made publicly available through a joint effort between the American Dental Association and the Centers for Disease Control claims "for most cities, every $1 invested in community water fluoridation saves $38 in dental treatment costs" and suggests that fluoridation means lower taxes and lower health insurance premiums for the general public (CDC, 2006). The CDC bases these figures, adjusted for current dollar value, on a 2001 economic analysis of fluoridation published in the *Journal of Public Health Dentistry* (CDC, 2015). This analysis determined "the annual per-person cost savings resulting from fluoridation ranged from $15.95 in very small communities to $18.62 in large communities" (Griffin, 2001). The CDC explains:

The analysis takes into account the costs of installing and maintaining necessary equipment and operating water plants, the expected effectiveness of fluoridation, estimates of expected cavities in non-fluoridated communities, treatment of cavities, and time lost visiting the dentist for treatment. (CDC, 2015).

V. What Are the Dental Health Benefits of Fluoride?

The consistent ingestion of fluoride has no benefits to the human body in any of the literature either for or against fluoridation, excepting cases where doctors administered high doses as a temporary treatment for specific ailments. Some sources warn of the health risks of ingesting fluoride and others claim ingestion at current municipal levels is safe. But *no one* touts any benefits of repeatedly ingesting fluoride.

The benefits of fluoride come from its lingering presence on teeth. Its contact with the tooth enamel provides the benefits. No dentist will argue this point. It is why mouthwash says to swish it and hold it on your teeth, spit it out, and avoid eating or drinking anything for a time. The benefits of fluoride derive from its presence on your teeth, not from digesting it in your body. Medical literature is clear on this point, and any family dentist can confirm it.

Fluoride versus the Real Cause of Tooth Decay. Tooth decay does not occur simply due to a lack of fluoride in drinking water. Tooth decay happens when sugar interacts with bacteria in the mouth. As the World Health Organization states in the *WHO Guidelines for Drinking-Water Quality*:

"The etiology of dental caries [tooth decay] involves the interplay on the tooth surface between certain oral bacteria and simple sugars (e.g. sucrose) derived from the diet. In the absence of those sugars in foods and drinks, dental caries will not be a public health problem. However where sugar consumption is high or is increasing, dental caries will be or will become a major public health problem unless there is appropriate intervention" (Lennon, 2004, p.1).

Fluoridation, therefore, is a measure designed to compensate for two things: one, a diet high in added sugar and, two, a level of personal dental hygiene inadequate to compensate for the lingering presence of sugar on one's teeth. As the WHO report makes clear, a low-sugar diet would contribute to a reduction in tooth decay. A dental hygiene regimen focused on removing those sugars before bonding with oral bacteria would also reduce tooth decay.

Many dentists speak out in favor of fluoridation because, especially in demographics with low incomes, dental hygiene is not maintained by parents and therefore not by their children. As Tucson dentist and advocate of fluoridation Dr. Philip Mooberry told the *Arizona Daily Star*, "The kids in my practice are decay-free, most of them. Who this affects is kids who don't get in to see the dentist" (Innes, 2014). This would be predominantly children from low-income families. Dentists hope the lack of adequate dental hygiene and regular care will be compensated for by keeping a low level of fluoride in the mouth due to drinking a city's tap water.

Dental Health Benefits of Topical Fluoride Use. The American Academy of Pedodontics published research by a team of dentists in 1982. The study examined reductions in tooth decay using different concentrations of sodium fluoride-based mouthrinse. "The study was conducted in eight Polk County, FL, high schools... where water fluoride level was less than 0.3 ppm," and it compared reduction rates between daily and weekly rinsing, too (Ringleberg, 1982, p. 305). Over a period of two years, students received a rinse in their classrooms, monitored by a teacher.

This simple classroom activity showed significantly reduced rates of tooth decay from both daily and weekly rinses, and from both 0.2% mouthrinse and 0.05% mouthrinse. (0.05% is the sodium fluoride concentration listed on over-the-counter product ACT Anticavity Fluoride Rinse.) The group with the greatest reduction used 0.05% mouthrinse daily. This easy, daily routine resulted in a difference of 46.2% fewer signs of tooth decay after two years. However, Dr. Ringleberg, the study's leading author and an assistant public health director at the time, noted similar studies in the literature showed "no significant differences between the effect of daily and weekly rinses." He concluded the differences between frequencies of use were "not sufficient to recommend daily rather than weekly doses." Dr.

Ringleberg points out this fact for schools and administrators considering a school-based fluoride rinse program, noting "the cost-effectiveness of a weekly rinse is better." In other words, even a single weekly fluoride rinse creates a marked reduction in tooth decay.

VI. What Are the Health Risks of Ingesting Fluoride?

Fluoride and Prozac. Fluoride is a negatively charged ion of the element fluorine. Fluorine is found on our planet in mineral forms where it combines in molecules with other elements, such as the bond between one calcium and two fluorine atoms in fluorite (CaF_2). Fluorine is "never found in a free state in nature, but always in combination with other elements as fluoride compounds" (BFS, 2015). Bonded sets of fluorine atoms do appear in chemicals, such as the group of three fluorine atoms making up part of the fluoxetine molecule ($C_{17}H_{18}F_3NO$). Fluoxetine hydrochloride is better known by its brand name, Prozac, and other branded and generic forms of the chemical sold as a drug. This explains the chemical truth behind claims about fluoride's role as an ingredient in Prozac.

Claims that the chemicals in fluoridation systems have the same mood-altering and serotonin reuptake-inhibiting effects as the chemicals in Prozac, however, have no supporting research. It would be a mistake to assume a single element determines the properties of all the different molecules where it can be found. For example, pure sodium reacts with water by exploding quite powerfully. A potentially fatal force could result from just a handful of pure sodium thrown into water. But when bonded to chlorine, sodium makes a table salt which dissolves peacefully in water. This example should make it clear that fluorine's well-documented presence in Prozac does mean one can assume every substance with fluorine will act like Prozac.

Fluoride and the Thyroid. Although the World Health Organization believes fluoridation is a beneficial public health policy, they do not deny its dangers. Their report on fluoride in drinking water says the "adverse effects... range from mild dental fluorosis [a discoloration of the tooth enamel] to crippling skeletal fluorosis... a significant cause of morbidity in a number of regions around the world" (WHO, 2006). Skeletal fluorosis manifests as increased bone fractures, joint pain, and impaired mobility. Even those who claim fluoridation is safe cannot deny certain levels of exposure to fluoride through ingestion are not safe for humans.

When a citizen concerned about the effect of fluoride on her thyroid brought the matter to city council in Phoenix, she was not alone in this concern. Fluorine's ability to damage the parathyroid glands and lead to hyperparathyroidism is known from examining patients with skeletal fluorosis. As far back as 1973, a *British Medical Journal* article found five patients of twenty with skeletal fluorosis also had "clear evidence of secondary hyperparathyroidism" (Teotia, 1973, p. 637).

On the other hand, symptoms of hyperthyroidism "were completely relieved by administration of fluorine in 6 of 15 patients; tachycardia was stopped and tremor disappeared with four to eight weeks and loss of weight was stopped" in a 1958 Swiss study which administered, orally and by injection, very large doses of fluoride, as high as 20mg in a single dose (Galetti, 1958). The researchers believed the results stemmed from fluoride's ability to inhibit the "thyroid iodide-concentrating mechanism" and this inhibitory effect on the thyroid took place when iodide levels in the blood were low, but not when iodide was plentiful in blood.

Either way, both sides of the fluoride debate can agree that fluoride can affect the thyroid and parathyroid glands. A high dose administered by a medical professional in a clinical setting may effectively treat specific symptoms, but uncontrolled doses can be clearly dangerous. The World Health Organization does not include thyroid concerns in its 2006 publication *Fluoride in Drinking Water*, though it does believe the studies it reviewed show no cause for concern about fluoride in relation to cancer (p. 34), and no cause for concern about damage to reproductive organs (p. 31) or DNA mutation (p. 31).

Dosage. The World Health organization, like the U.S. Department of Health & Human Services, believes their recommended fluoridation levels make ingestion of fluoride safe and, in fact, beneficial due to a reduction in tooth decay. The exposures to levels of fluoride which cause significant harm are greater than the levels recommended for municipalities. The message is clear. Fluoride in large amounts or over long periods of time can be harmful to human health, though citizens may drink it at low concentrations.

Most reports of fluoride damage to the body take place at levels far above the EPA's Maximum Contaminant Level. But to put the EPA's figure of 4 mg/L into perspective, the same MCL applies to bleach. The EPA sets an enforceable level for chlorine, the disinfectant ingredient in bleach, at the same level as fluoride: 4mg/L (EPA, 2015). In other words, the recommended levels of fluoride in city water are just as safe to drink as bleach diluted to the same level. This does not necessarily mean that either chemical is "safe."

VII. Policy Options for Citizens.

Citizens concerned about fluoridation should seek change through public referendum. In areas of state-mandated fluoridation, this may be a greater task than in areas where individual municipalities choose their own fluoridation policy. Fluoridation has far too much popular support currently, not to mention federal support from the CDC and international support from the WHO, to expect a federal initiative to have any political feasibility.

However, the question of whether or not to fluoridate always arrives at city council or on the ballot as an either/or proposition. Either we add the chemicals, or we do not. The concerns of dentists and parent groups are never met with an alternative solution. As Boulder's recent example demonstrates, many voters want to maintain the dental health benefits of fluoridation. A simple repeal of their fluoridation policy offers no new policy in its place. Without an alternative that pleases dentists and parents, the effort to repeal fluoridation with a public referendum can prove wasted effort.

Therefore, the anti-fluoridation movement faces a considerable hurdle which often goes unnoticed amidst the arguments over whether or not fluoride is "safe," or if its benefits are "real." These questions politicize and polarize the discussion. An alternative policy which removed the risks of ingesting fluoride while making its topical benefits widely available, especially to low-income families and citizens, would instead unify the discussion. With this in mind, what policy options could citizens offer as alternatives?

Elements of a Comprehensive Alternative. Dr. Ringelberg's study of daily and weekly fluoride rinses in classrooms provides a model for a policy which could replace fluoridation. A school-based program would reach children without adequate dental care at home, the group which most concerns dentists who advocate fluoridation. A policy targeting only schools in low-income areas would still reach the children of greatest concern and reduce the overall cost of the policy. City funds currently spent on purchasing hazardous chemicals from out-of-state suppliers could be redirected towards a school-based fluoride rinse program. Cities making decisions to begin fluoridation would have even more funding for a program, as they would not bear the costs of constructing and staffing new facilities or purchasing equipment. For a city like Tucson, where infrastructure challenges prevent a fluoridation citizens requested, an alternative program could meet their needs.

Such a program would provide benefits no fluoridation policy offers. The daily or weekly routine of rinsing makes dental hygiene part of children's lives. It builds long-term habits. It raises their awareness that their teeth may be something worth taking extra care of. The programs offer an opportunity to educate about dental hygiene and its importance, through presentations or literature. Informational literature distributed to children and parents as part of the program would raise community awareness. Fluoridating water provides dental benefits but zero education. Fluoridation does not change behavior or move our culture any closer towards healthy dental hygiene habits. Education will.

Purchasing and distributing fluoride mouthwash to schools may appear less cost-effective than buying hydrofluorosilicic acid by the gallon. But a comprehensive public health program involves communities. A school-based rinse program provides an opportunity for retailers to subsidize its costs. A branded mouthwash company might welcome the opportunity to provide its product to schools at a reduced cost or even no cost as an advertising and marketing opportunity. Manufacturers of fluoride toothpastes, toothbrushes, and dental floss would welcome an opportunity to sponsor a daily or weekly dental hygiene program in schools, especially if they could distribute branded promotional items as part of the program. Providing the tools for dental care from program sponsors would especially benefit low-income families and families in crisis.

One city's perfect solution may not be the ideal policy for another city. In a city with few or no low-income residents, an awareness and education campaign may be all that is needed to make fluoridation unnecessary. Where people have the means and the education to adopt a topical fluoride program personally, distribution of fluoride rinses at schools could be an unnecessary expense. Therefore, citizen groups seeking to craft alternative policy should consider the basic elements of a comprehensive strategy, but tailor them to fit the needs of each unique community.

Such a comprehensive policy would involve the most threatened citizens with their communities and schools, open a public dialogue, and provide opportunities for everyone to contribute to positive change. Fluoridation is far from comprehensive, as it is a benefit received passively and without any awareness or behavior change. If anything, fluoridation encourages poor dental hygiene habits by treating citizens as too simple-minded to take care of themselves. School-based rinse programs would bring the same benefits as fluoridation while working to bring about a culture of dental hygiene where further fluoridation would be unnecessary.

No single tactic can comprehensively solve a public health problem like tooth decay, not when the causes are many and the solution which works in one case may not work in another. As other public health programs demonstrate, such as the recent tobacco control and packaging laws in Australia, citizens need information and support at multiple places and multiple times to effect large-scale changes in behavior. As researchers from the International Tobacco Control Project concluded in regards to the effectiveness of campaigns to reduce tobacco smoking in Australia, the policies are effective because they are part of a comprehensive set of policies aimed at multiple media channels and including warnings both at the point of sale and on packaging (Li, 2012, p. 430). Comprehensiveness matters.

Options for Those Who Cannot Stop Fluoridation. In communities where the majority favors fluoridation, policy should make some allowance for those who object. It seems contrary to fundamental American ideals such as liberty and self-determination to force people to accept a known hazardous chemical in their water, regardless of what benefits it may have. An option to buy bottled, purified water is open to anyone who can afford the cost, but it does nothing to address the use of fluoridated water for bathing, hygiene, or cooking, nor the needs of those low-income families who may find the cost a burden.

Fortunately, one state has already come up with a politically feasible and fair policy. According to a 2000 review of fluoridation laws in all 50 states, Georgia "specifies that any person deemed allergic to fluoridated water who finds it necessary, upon advice of a physician or approval of the Department of Human Resources, to buy a defluoridation device may count it as a tax deductible item" (qtd. in Juneau, 2006, p. 98). This policy still places the initial cost of opting out of fluoridation on the individual objector, but it offers a corresponding reduction in tax liability. A tax deduction could easily be extended to any resident who objects to fluoride and wants to install a filtration system to remove it. While Georgia's measure is laudable, it should go farther in offering the deduction to anyone and remove the administrative hurdles of proving an allergy or seeking approval. An objection to drinking toxic chemicals should be sufficient.

A truly egalitarian policy of this nature would include an additional allowance for those who only claim the standard deduction on their income taxes. After all, a tax credit is only good to someone who itemizes their deductions, and the people who do not itemize tend to be lower income people. To avoid placing an undue burden on low-income citizens for opting out of community-mandated fluoride, the tax credit could be made available to all taxpayers regardless of itemizing their deductions or not, much like the Earned Income Credit and other tax credits any tax filer may calculate individually on their return.

VIII. Conclusion.

Anti-fluoridation efforts have failed for two main reasons. First, the number of unsupported claims and wild accusations harm the efforts by exchanging controversy for hard facts. Citizens with legitimate concerns about consuming a hazardous waste product find themselves associated with "tin foil hats" and "conspiracy theories." Second, when the seriousness of their claims becomes a matter of discourse in city councils and public ballots, no alternative policy is provided for concerned dentists and parents. To succeed in removing the toxic chemicals of the fluoridation process from water supplies, anti-fluoride activists need to find a way to provide the topical benefits of fluoride to communities. A school-based program of supervised daily or even weekly fluoride rinses would bring the benefits of fluoride to communities, and it would provide a touch point for other comprehensive measures for education and awareness. If sugar and dental hygiene are the real culprits behind tooth decay, a comprehensive policy would address them directly rather than indirectly through addition of hazardous chemicals to the water supply.

References

ACT. (2015). "ACT Anticavity drug facts."
http://www.actoralcare.com/products/act-anticavity/

Activists for Truth and Liberty. (June 16, 2014). "Dr. Paul Connett, PhD speaks to Dallas City Council on June 11, 2014." Video
https://youtu.be/xguPD85-BH4

Bowers, Becky. (October 6, 2011). "Truth about fluoride doesn't include Nazi myth." *Politifact Florida (Tampa Bay Times, Miami Herald).*
http://www.politifact.com/florida/statements/2011/oct/06/crit
ics-water-fluoridation/truth-about-fluoride-doesnt-include-
nazi-myth/

British Fluoridation Society. (2015). "Technical aspects of water fluoridation."
http://www.bfsweb.org/facts/tech_aspects/chemsmanufac.ht
m

Centers for Disease Control and Prevention (CDC). (2015). "Cost savings of community water fluoridation."
http://www.cdc.gov/fluoridation/factsheets/cost.htm

Centers for Disease Control and Prevention (CDC) and American Dental Association (ADA). (2006). "Water fluoridation: nature's way to prevent tooth decay."
http://www.cdc.gov/fluoridation/pdf/natures_way.pdf

City of Boulder, Colorado. (2015). "Inquire Boulder: fluoride."
https://user.govoutreach.com/boulder/faq.php?cid=23302

City of Phoenix Water Services Department. (May 7, 2012). "Q & A fluoride" (listed as Fluoride use in tap water on website).
https://www.phoenix.gov/waterservicessite/Documents/wsdfl
uoride070512b.pdf

City of Phoenix Water Services Department, Environmental Division. (2015). "2014 typical water analysis." PDF retrieved via email to the author from the department.

Connett, Paul. (2004). Fifty reasons to oppose fluoridation. *Medical Veritas, 1*, 70-80. http://www.waterskraus.com/pdf/50%20Reasons%20to%20Oppose%20Fluoridation.pdf

Environmental Protection Agency (EPA). (2015). "Basic information about fluoride in drinking water." http://water.epa.gov/drink/contaminants/basicinformation/fluoride.cfm

Environmental Protection Agency (EPA). (2015). "Basic information about disinfectants in drinking water: chloramine, chlorine and chlorine dioxide." http://water.epa.gov/drink/contaminants/basicinformation/disinfectants.cfm

Environmental Protection Agency (EPA). (January, 2011). "Questions and answers on fluoride." http://water.epa.gov/lawsregs/rulesregs/regulatingcontaminants/sixyearreview/upload/2011_Fluoride_QuestionsAnswers.pdf

Espericueta, Pete. (May 7, 2015). *Phone interview with author.*

Forsythe, Jerilyn. (August 16, 2012). "One woman's curiosity reopens water fluoridation debate in Phoenix." *Cronkite News.* http://cronkitenewsonline.com/2012/08/one-womans-curiosity-reopens-water-fluoridation-debate-in-phoenix/

Fluoride Action Network. (2015). "Water fluoridation: fluoridation chemicals." *FluorideAlert.org.* http://fluoridealert.org/issues/water/fluoridation-chemicals/

Galetti, P and Joyet, G. (October, 1958). "Effect of fluorine on thyroidal iodine metabolism in hyperthyroidism." *Journal of Clinical Endocrinology & Metabolism, 18*(10), 1102-1110. Reprinted text http://www.slweb.org/galletti.html

Gardiner, Dustin. (September 11, 2012). "Phoenix panel decides to continue fluoridating drinking water." *AZCentral* (The Republic). http://archive.azcentral.com/community/ahwatukee/articles/2012/09/11/20120911phoenix-panel-decides-continue-fluoridating-drinking-water.html

Griffin, S. O., et. al. (Spring, 2001). "An economic evaluation of community water fluoridation." *Journal of Public Health Dentistry, 61*(2), 78-86. Abstract: http://www.ncbi.nlm.nih.gov/pubmed/11474918

Innes, Stephanie. (November 2, 2014). "Cavities again? Blame the Tucson water system." *Tucson.com* (Arizona Daily Star). http://tucson.com/news/science/health-med-fit/cavities-again-blame-the-tucson-water-system/article_33d26ed3-2fb0-5385-b14c-e97630237f4e.html

Isquith, Elias. (December 2, 2014). "These pseudo-religious people who I find laughable: Jesse Ventura talks Republicans, Nazis and running for president." *Salon.* http://www.salon.com/2014/12/02/these_pseudo_religious_people_who_i_find_laughable_jesse_ventura_talks_republicans_nazis_and_running_for_president/

Juneau Fluoride Study Commission. (July 11, 2006). "Report to the Assembly of the City and Borough of Juneau: Exhibit C Summaries of Actions on Fluoridation in Other Jurisdictions." http://fluoridealert.org/wp-content/uploads/juneau.2006.ages94-110_Exhibit_C.pdf

Lennon, Michael A. (September, 2004). "Rolling revision of the WHO guidelines for drinking-water quality: fluoride (Draft)." *World Health Organization.* http://www.who.int/water_sanitation_health/dwq/nutfluoride.pdf

Lennon, Michael A. (September, 2006). "One in a million: the first community trial of water fluoridation." *Bulletin of the World Health Organization, 84*(9), 759-760. http://www.ncbi.nlm.nih.gov/pmc/articles/PMC2627472/pdf/17128347.pdf

Li, Lin, et. al. (Feb. 2012). "The association between exposure to point-of-sale anti-smoking warnings and smokers' interest in quitting and quit attempts: findings from the International Tobacco Control Four Country Survey." *Addiction, 107*(2), 425-433. DOI: 10.1111/j.1360-0443.2011.03668.x

Linenfelser, Bret. (May 6, 2015). *Phone interview with author.*

Mercola, Joseph. (July 1, 2014). "Expert testimony: how your drinking water may be damaging your brain." http://articles.mercola.com/sites/articles/archive/2014/07/01/water-supply-fluoridation.aspx#_edn1

Mosaic. (2015). "Hydrofluorosilicic acid (FSA or HFS)." http://www.mosaicco.com/products/industrial_products_hfs.htm

Mosaic. (2015). *Material Safety Data Sheet: hydrofluorosilicic acid.* http://www.mosaicco.com/documents/Hydrofluosilicic_Acid_MSDS_03Jan14.pdf

Mosaic CropNutrition. (2015). *CropNutrition.com.*

Ringleberg, M. L., et. al. (1982). "Effectiveness of different concentrations and frequencies of sodium fluoride mouthrinse." *The American Association of Pedodontics,* 4(4): 305-308. http://www.aapd.org/assets/1/25/Ringelberg-04-04.pdf

ScienceLab. (2015). *Material Safety Data Sheet: sodium fluoride.* http://www.sciencelab.com/msds.php?msdsId=9927595

ScienceLab. (2015). *Material Safety Data Sheet: sodium silicofluoride.* http://www.sciencelab.com/msds.php?msdsId=9925037

Teotia, S., et. al. (1973). "Secondary hyperparathyroidism in patients with endemic skeletal fluorosis." *BMJ,* 1, 637-640. http://www.ncbi.nlm.nih.gov/pmc/articles/PMC1588649/pdf/brmedj01547-0019.pdf

Thatcher Company. (2015). "Thatcher agriculture: agriculture product list." http://tchem.com/industries/agriculture/

US Department of Health & Human Services (HHS). (September,1993.) "Fluoridation census: Arizona." http://www.fluoridealert.org/wp-content/uploads/arizona_census.pdf

US Department of Health and Human Services (HHS). (April 27, 2015). "HHS issues final recommendation for community water fluoridation: Adjusted level seeks to maintain dental health benefits of fluoride." http://www.hhs.gov/news/press/2015pres/04/20150427a.html

US Department of Health and Human Services (HHS). (September, 2003). "Toxicological profile for fluorides, hydrogen fluoride, and fluorine." http://www.atsdr.cdc.gov/toxprofiles/tp11.pdf. Summary page at http://www.atsdr.cdc.gov/toxprofiles/tp.asp?id=212&tid=38

Wilonsky, Robert. (January 28, 2015). "After year of debate, Dallas City Council votes not to remove fluoride from city's water supply." *The Dallas Morning News: City Hall Blog.* http://cityhallblog.dallasnews.com/2015/01/after-year-of-debate-dallas-city-council-votes-not-to-remove-fluoride-from-citys-water-supply.html/

World Health Organization. (2006). *Fluoride in drinking-water* by J. Fawell, et. al. London, UK: IWA Publishing. http://www.who.int/water_sanitation_health/publications/fluoride_drinking_water_full.pdf

World Health Organization (WHO). (2004). "Fluoride in Drinking-water: Background document for development of WHO Guidelines for Drinking-water Quality." http://www.who.int/water_sanitation_health/dwq/chemicals/fluoride.pdf

About the Author

Matthew earned a Bachelor of Interdisciplinary Studies in Public Administration in 2014 from Northern Arizona University. He continues his studies at Fort Hays State University where he is working towards a Master of Liberal Studies in Public Administration. He studies public policy as it relates to patents, international trade agreements, health, and telecommunications in the Internet age.

Matthew enjoys helping other authors self-publish their work. He supports authors, speakers, and business professionals in creating books that provide positive, practical information to improve people's lives and make a difference in our world. Their recent projects have contributed to greater awareness in the fields of business leadership, interpersonal communication, personal finance, and health & nutrition.

www.ingramcontent.com/pod-product-compliance
Lightning Source LLC
Chambersburg PA
CBHW050118280326
41933CB00010B/1152